W9-DEB-011

careers

in **computer graphics & animation**:
Gardner's Guide Series

Garth Gardner, Ph.D.

GGC Inc./*Publishing*

Fairfax, Virginia

Editorial inquiries concerning this book should be e-mailed to:
info@ggcinc.com

www.gogardner.com

Copyright © 2001,2003 GGC, Inc. All rights reserved

No part of this book may be reproduced, stored in a retrieval
system, or transmitted in any form or by any other means—
electronic, mechanical, photocopying, recording, or otherwise—
except for citations of data for scholarly or reference purposes,
with full acknowledgment of title, edition, and publisher, and
written notification to GGC/Publishing prior to such use.

GGC/Publishing is a department of, and *Gardner's Guide* is a
trademark of GGC, Inc.

Library of Congress Cataloging-in-Publication Data:

Gardner, Garth.
    Careers in Computer Graphics and Animation/
Garth Gardner.
        p. cm. — (Gardner's guide series)
Cover title: Careers in computer graphics & animation.
Includes index.

Summary: Summarizes positions and professions in the fields of
computer graphics, design, and animation, discussing position
titles, potential salaries, and related information obtained
through interviews with professionals in these fields.
ISBN 0-9661075-2-7

        1.   Computer animation—Vocational guidance—Juvenile
literature.
        2.   Computer graphics—Vocational guidance—Juvenile
literature. [1. Computer animation—Vocational guidance. 2.
Computer graphics—Vocational guidance. 3. Vocational
guidance.] I. Title: Careers in computer graphics & animation.
II. Title. III. Series.
TR897.7 .G37 2001
006.6'96'023—dc21

                                                2001004020

Printed in Canada

Table of Contents

Acknowledgement

The careers listed in this book are the result of a number of individuals who worked to make this project possible. I am truly grateful to Leah Tomaino for our discussions that planted the seed for this project and for the ground work she provided. Dina Patel for her assistants in researching the fundamental issues and questions, and Ryan Bell for his opinions and research assistance. Marie Wright and Lisa Lotti for the photographs used in the book. To Evan Rosenfeld for his editorial insights and assistance. To Carrie Tucker for her overall assistance. To Nic Banks for his service as art director on this project.

I am truly thankful to the many practitioners who took the time to be interviewed for this project, and to the studios for giving them the time off to contribute to this project. Thanks to the companies: Curious Pictures, R/GA, Digital Division, Media Vision, Henninger Media, Blue Sky Studios, and Waveworks Digital Media for providing the environment for the photographers. Thanks to my colleagues and students at George Mason University for providing me with a teaching and learning environment. And to the participating schools: Academy of Art College, The Dave School, Full Sail, Pratt, Art Institute of Southern California, School of Communication Arts, and Cogswell Polytechincal College for their continued support.

About the Author

Garth Gardner, Ph.D. is a professor of animation and multimedia. He has taught and lectured at several universities including The Ohio State University, William Paterson University, University of California Los Angeles, Fashion Institute of Technology, Florida A&M University, University of Southern California, Xavier University, and George Mason University. Dr. Gardner has spoken at numerous high schools and is the author of several books on the subject of computer graphics and animation. He is a graduate of San Francisco State University and The Ohio State University.

Foreword

Unlimited Opportunities

One of the biggest challenges for a student entering college is declaring a major. For the student of the arts this is compounded by the fact that the arts themselves have various areas of specialty. For the student concerned about making a secure living after graduation, there is no longer a need to struggle to make a decision between the arts and other careers. Career choice can now be safely narrowed to the traditional fine arts and technological arts. Both require the same foundation courses, and both are mediums for personal expression; however, today, with the advent of the computer, technological art has become the most stable form of art with regard to income. The artist who has embraced technology is seeing the light at the end of the tunnel.

That light comes in the form of financial security for an artist, and respect from the general public as a whole. Today technology artists such as computer animations, designers, and multimedia practitioners are commanding the salaries of the scientists, engineers, and even doctors. With only a four-year degree, a summer internship or two, and true dedication to their art, these media artists can earn a salary that they can comfortably live on. And when the going gets rough, if it ever does, they can freelance on the side. The low cost of computer equipment today means that they can afford to furnish a home office or start a business. There are many career opportunities in the field of computer graphics and animation. But before inviting everyone to join the field of computer graphics and animation, let's add the negative.

Yes there are some negatives to this new media field that fuses art and technology. Artists have learned that they must adapt readily to the changes in technology, and have surrendered to being perpetual students of technology. Secondly, the bulk of artwork today is done for commercial interests. Gone are the days when artist did work for the purpose of self-expression, or to make a statement to society, or because they like the color red. The media artist does what he or she does because he or she is being paid, or because the Director chooses that color red. Part of the result is that that the artists are able to receive credits at the end of blockbuster movies.

Media artwork is usually the product of group activities involving hundreds specialists. Take for example the area of animation, which is a complex area to define, even before computers. Traditional animation alone comprises involves several areas of specialization: stop-motion, clay animation, paper manipulation, glass animation, cel animation, and the list continues to grow. Computer technology has introduced two-dimensional and three-dimensional computer animation. And within each of these areas of specialization, the production requires several artists, producers, managers, Directors, and postproduction practitioners, each doing their part to create one collaborative art project. Whether working on a feature film, a multimedia project, or an animation, team dynamics will be involved in the production.

For the students that wish to join those teams, this book is written for you. This book explores some of the areas of specialty within the new media field. It defines the industry jargon and reviews the career titles that the studios seek to employ. It is written specifically for that student who needs to examine the professional possibilities of the field before settling for one choice or another. This book is the starting point for defining the many opportunities that are available to the beginner and to those who seek to advance their careers.

Fine art is never without technology and the computer is just the latest technological tool that the artist has embraced. This tool however has given them great leverage over other areas. Master the tools and art and you can manifest your own destiny. What are some of the popular career paths in computer graphics and animation? How can I prepare for a career in this area? What is the income potential for entry level? These are just some of the questions that are answered in this book.

Chapter Structure

The first 11 chapters of this book define over 130 different position titles. For many positions interviews with professionals were included to provide more depth to job descriptions. Chapter 12 and 13 offers advice to students based on information collected from over 75 interviews. The appendix section of the book lists company contact information, suggested books and magazines for further reading, and a glossary of terms.

Each of the first 11 chapters begins with a general sections describing one of the respective fields. Within these descriptions readers will find general information about job responsibilities, educational requirements, and salary.

Responsibilities: This is a general description of what it takes to get into the careers described in the chapter. This section describes how the various areas in relate to each other. It is an overview of the field that introduces the specific areas.

Education: This section of the book covers the education and training required to qualify for a position within the category of careers.

Salary Information: This section of each chapter provides a general salary bracket for a person in this line of career.

Following each chapter's general description readers will find listings for the available areas of employment. This second section of the chapter offers specifics about what can be expected of people working in a given job area. It is important to note that some of these positions are very specific. Others are more general positions, and are thus less clearly defined. At most smaller companies employees usually do several jobs, thus blurring the boundaries of their career titles.

Note: At the end of each area description readers will find an estimated entry-level salary range. Salary varies according to location and size of a company. Often larger companies will pay more or closer to the market value as they must remain competitive in attracting the best talent. However this salary range is just for a ballpark measure of what one can make in the field. The amounts printed in this section represent an average of what the larger studios may pay in 2001. Future salaries in the market may differ. Entry-level is defined as the salary that can be earned by a college graduate with internship experience in their area of employment. In the case of such careers as Executive Producers, and other management positions, these jobs are rarely given to the inexperience college graduate; however, this book provides an estimate of what qualified persons in these professions can expect to earn in their first year of production at an established small to large studio.

Following the area descriptions, the third section of each chapter presents a series of interviews. This is where you can read about the life of actual job practitioners. The information is the first hand response to interview questions. Responses address such topics as: an average day on the job, education required for a job, salary, and recommended sources for further information.

Overview of Chapters

Chapter 1: Animators

This chapter examines the role of the Animator at traditional and computer animation studios. Various animation techniques, from stop-motion, to cel animation, to computer animation, are discussed in this chapter.

Chapter 2: Modelers

This chapter explains the role of modelers. Three-dimensional Animation must start with a model. Sometimes the models are built with clay, and other times the models are built on the computer through the use of three-dimensional computer graphics. In this chapter a few of these modeling positions are defined.

Chapter 3: Designers

This chapter explores some of the design positions that now use computers as a medium for visualizing the final results. It looks at some of the general areas of design, such as graphic design that have now been incorporated into the computer graphics field.

Chapter 4: Creative and Technical Directors

The computer graphics field requires both technical knowledge and creative inspiration. This chapter looks at the contributions of Creative Directors and Technical Directors who often work closely with one another to determine what can be accomplished on projects in an allotted time span.

From top to bottom: Traditional Animator at Curious; Model from Curious Pictures' A Little Curious for HBO; Interior Design Project; Pictures Producer at R/GA

Chapter 5: Supporting Artist

This chapter examines the roles traditional fine artists often play in the production of a computer graphics project. Often involved in the planning stages of the production, these artists often find employment under titles such as Character Designers and Painters.

Chapter 6: Editors

This chapter explores the roles of postproduction practitioners such as Video Editors, Print Editors, and Compositors. Both linear-analog and non-linear-digital career opportunities are covered in this chapter.

Chapter 7: Programmers and Engineers

From Web Developers to Software Developers, this chapter defines the career options for technical practitioners in the art of computer graphics and animation. These computer scientists and engineers range from individuals who write scripts or code on the computer to aid an artist in creating a unique effect, to those who write programs for video games.

Chapter 8: Managers/Producers/CEOs

Managers, Producers, and CEO's are the individuals who often finance and oversee productions. This chapter defines the production titles often given to Company Executives on a project.

Chapter 9: Educators and Trainers

This chapter describes the roles and responsibilities of Educators including College Professors, Industrial Trainers, Studio Trainers, and others whose careers may involve teaching people media technologies.

From top to bottom: Storyboard from Curious Pictures' A Little Curious for HBO; Digital Division's Technical Writer; Video Engineer at Media Vision; Project Manager at Media Visions; Digital Division's Training Center

Chapter 10: Writers

Having an understanding of media technologies is important for all writers, as professionals may be required to upload information directly to the internet, code information, and/or create hyperlinks. This chapter examines the roles of Writers in this technological field.

Chapter 11: Camera Operators

This chapter looks at the traditional roles of some Camera Operators. With the advent of such tools as digital cameras and digital audio mixers, the audio-video field has widened the definition of computer graphics.

Chapter 12: Advice to Beginners

This chapter solicits feedback from practitioners regarding the question: What advice would you give to students preparing for a career in your field? The goal of this chapter is to provide concrete first hand information to help guide students preparing for the various areas of this field.

Chapter 13: The Portfolio Matters

This chapter looks at practitioners' direct response to the question: What do you look for in a portfolio?

From top to bottom: Digital Division's Technical Writer; Alias|Wavefront's Poster for the animation short *Bingo* directed by Chris Landreth

Introduction

A Brief Introduction to the Production Process

The are three stages to media production: preproduction, production, and postproduction. This section gives a brief overview of the entire production process from concept to finish. Knowledge of how the production process actually works can yield a better understanding of each professional role.

During preproduction media Producers acquire a concept, and oversee the planning of a project. During this stage producers

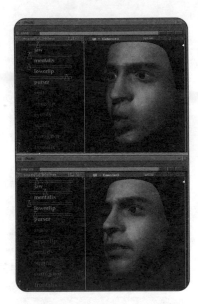

Alias|Wavefront Maya's User Interface. A still from *The End*, an animation short film directed by Chris Landreth

manage the writing, budgeting, and previsualization of a script. Production Designers continuously revise character and visual style during this phase. Usually a storyboard is drawn to layout how the project will look upon its completion.

During the production stage the production staff engages in the hands-on creation of the product itself (i.e., the feature film, animation sequence, etc.). On film projects, the cameraperson and crew will actually complete all photography during this phase. On animation projects, illustrators, modelers, and engineers will work together to complete all of their motion sequences.

During Postproduction the final output is nearing completion. The postproduction staff manipulates the results of Production Artists into one coherent whole. Postproduction practitioners may include video editors, who resequence pictures, and sound mixers, who create assemblages of audio clips.

Large production facilities employ hundreds of practitioners to complete the tasks necessary during these three production stages (pre, pro, post). The following is just one example of the way a small, three-dimensional, computer animation production goes through the production pipeline. The process of producing animation is slightly different than the process used for other media projects, but there are some basic similarities from one field to the next.

Prepoduction of a 3D Computer Animation:
Preproduction typically starts with a script. The script is written by someone within the animation studio. The storyboard is then created to visualize the script. Characters are designed. The animation Stylist creates the concept artwork for the look of the animation. If the project requires complex digital modeling, maquettes or miniatures may be built. The research and

development team may begin the process of writing proprietary software and developing user-interfaces to expedite foreseeable challenges in the production of the story. Test animation may also be carried out at this planning stage. If required, voices may be previewed at this stage of the production.

Production of a 3D Computer Animation:

In the production stage is the majority of the work is done. The modeling team builds models in accordance with designs form the Character Designer. Riggers then set up all completed models for animation. If maquettes are used they are digitized into the computer and are converted into three-dimensional graphic models. The animation team brings the characters to life by animating the various scenes, cameras, and environments in accordance with the script and storyboard. The technical directing team resolves any technical issues involved with the software or hardware. Once completed the animation goes to the lighting and texture practitioners who are responsible for assigning color and lighting to models in accordance with script specifications.

Postproduction of a 3D Computer Animation:

During this stage the animation is composited, or layered, with other parts of the scene. The lighting is corrected. Everything is rendered, or finalized, on the computer, and then the motion sequences are edited. Adding sound is one of the final steps in the postproduction process. Background sound and sound effects are added to the edited motion sequences to create the final project.

Chapter 1
Animators

An Animator is an artist who makes inanimate objects appear mobile. He or she uses computers and photography to give artwork the illusion of movement. An Animator studies and brings graphics and action to life. He or she is basically someone capable of analyzing motion, breaking the motion down into individual components, and then recreating the motion as necessary. In a traditional animation, also called cel animation, environment the Animator is the person responsible for drawing the moving characters.

There are two main categories of animation: two-dimensional (2D) and three-dimensional (3D) animation. These categories cans be broken down into two overriding techniques: traditional (or classical)

Sleepy Guy a short animation created by PDI.

animation, and digital (or computer) animation. For example, a 2D traditional animation technique is the classical cel animation of early Walt Disney Films. An example of 3D traditional animation is the clay animation found in Gumby. On the computer side, 2D animation is much more difficult to spot in every day television programming, because it is often used to mimic traditional animation techniques. However most Disney feature films today are done digitally, that is to say that the 2D characters and the backgrounds are drawn, colored and developed solely on the computer. In the case of 3D computer animation, the examples are much more apparent. A good example is that of Disney/Pixar's Toy Story. In this film the computer was used to create the entire production. Animators are employed in various areas including film and television, videogames, Web animation, and forensic animation.

Artist works on HBO's *A Little Curious* at Curious Pictures

Responsibilities

The Animator creates a series of drawings, or manipulates 3D computer models or objects to form the illusion of motion. The Animator, whether working with 3D computer or 2D cel, functions as a member of a team. Their duties may include animating a singular character from a selection of objects within a given scene. Independent Animators usually work alone or in a smaller group. Working independently, one Animator may be required to animate an entire scene by him or her self. At large studios, Animators are given less creative freedom. They are asked by the Animation Supervisor to create in a specific manner, to meet the vision of the Creative Director. When working on a film they are often required to show the daily progression of the animation to the Director and production crew. The clips they show the Director and crew are called "Dailies". At daily sessions the Director has a chance to critique the animation and suggest changes.

Education

Animators in the cel and traditional animation areas should have a Bachelor of Arts degree in traditional animation. Those interested in 3D traditional animation should take classes in sculpture, ceramics, and lighting in addition to those courses suggested for traditional animation. It is important for all

Animators to learn to draw characters and develop a style of their own; however in the case of 2D Animators this is absolutely mandatory. Computer Animators should have a Bachelor of Arts degree in Animation or Computer Animation. Those interested in 3D computer animation must acquire the same experience recommended for 2D and 3D traditional Animators. In addition computer Animators should have a firm command of the tools of the computer trade. They must have a command of the software used for the animation, not to the point where they are committed to that software program for life, but to the point where they understand what it is capable of doing for a specific planned project. They should understand the basic principles of animation as it is applied to a digital 3D environment. Basic computer science classes such as C programming is recommended. All Animators should take classes such as dancing, acting, theater and drama, in addition to film or video production, script writing and the basic fine arts courses.

Entry-Level Salary Range

$20,000-$90,000. This will greatly depend on the size of the company, range of duties, area of specialty, and location of the company. Entry-level Animators doing computer animation in San Francisco Bay Area at a large studio such as Pixar may start around $45,000-$55,000, whereas computer Animators working at small studios in Florida on small budget productions may start at $20,000-$30,000.

Areas

Clay Animator

Clay Animators work with models made of clay to create stop motion animation. A Clay Animator is the person on the set who is moving and sculpting the characters, and operating the camera; in an independent or small studio environment the Clay

From top to bottom: Clay animation stills from Curious Pictures; Two stills from Alias|Wavefront's animation short *Bingo*

Animator may also design and build the characters from scratch, which sometimes requires doing a lot of sketching and drawing before sculpting begins. This is area is often referred to as "claymation," a term trademarked by Will Vinton. Entry-Level Salary Range: $35,000-$60,000.

Forensics Animator

Forensics Animators give life to scenes for medical illustrations, accident reconstructions, or simulations. They are responsible for gathering the information necessary for understanding an event. They put that information together into an animation, recreating terrains and surroundings. They actually calculate things such as angles of bullet shots or levels of visibility. They produce computer simulations and video/film composites that come as close as possible to demonstrating the factors attendant in a particular case. Entry-Level Salary Range: $35,000-$60,000.

3D Computer Animator

This Animator uses three-dimensional (3D) software applications to create and animate characters, objects, and effects. 3D Animators are responsible for choreography, timing, and acting of characters. These Animators also perfect the animation for objects, like blowing leaves, and effects, like undulating water. Entry-level 3D Animators would animate secondary characters, or object that move as a result of the main character's motion. The Animator uses the computer to create character skeletons, or wire frame models. Once these wire frame models are completed the Animator sets up key frames for the animation. The computer then calculates missing frames that are in-between these key frames. Entry-Level Salary Range: $35,000-$90,000.

Senior 3D Computer Animator

The Senior Animator's job at most studios is the same as that of the Animator. They both use artistry to create the nuances of motion, gesture and performance that bring characters to life. The senior position is usually given to Animators with over five years experience as an Animator. The position gives the Animator more creative licenses on projects. At some companies, the senior Animator may act as the Supervisor or Lead Animator on projects. Entry-Level Salary Range: $40,000-$70,000.

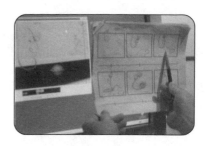

3D Computer Animator works from the storyboard at Curious Pictures.

Assistant Cel Animator

The chief function of the Assistant Cel Animator is to add to the rough drawings made by the Animator, leaving one or two in-betweens throughout for the In-betweener. Assistant Cel Animators also prepare scenes for pencil testing. After approval by the Director, the Assistant Cel Animator cleans up the roughs, checks the exposure sheets for errors, and computes pan moves before turning the work over to the In-betweener. As the Assistant gains expertise, the Animator gives him or her small bits of animation to do. Gradually this amount is increased, until the Assistant animates small scenes, then more important shots, finally graduating into a full-fledged Cel Animator. Entry-Level Salary Range: $20,000-$35,000. The salary often remains stable until the Assistant Animator advances.

Cel Animator

The Cel Animator is versatile in various styles of characters. The Cel Animator needs to know a great deal about Animation acting and practice. Fine draftsmanship is essential in this position, as is the ability to make funny drawings and actions. The Cel Animator should have knowledge of camera maneuverability in order to write comprehensive camera instructions. The Animator should have some executive ability

From top to bottom: 3D Computer Animator works from the storyboard; Traditional Animator at work; Stills of a stop-motion animator at work. All photos were taken at Curious Pictures.

in order to supervise the assistant Animator and in-between. Entry-Level Salary Range: $20,000-$60,000.

Stop-Motion Animator

Stop-motion is a traditional animation technique that dates back to the first decade of the 1900s. The Stop-Motion Animator creates animation through the use of three-dimensional ready-made objects such as dolls or created objects made from clay or latex, or through the use of two-dimensional objects such as paper cutouts. The stop motion Animator uses a film camera equipped with a single frame-recording device to record each single frame while manually manipulating the object after each exposure. When these singular photographs are projected in order—each image slightly adjusted from its predecessor— then the impression of movement is created. Entry-Level Salary Range: $20,000-$60,000.

Character Animator

The term Character Animator is given to an Animator who has the ability to use the tools of the trade to breath life into a 3D model to the extent that its actions reflect the exaggerated motion of a human or an animal. The Character Animator conceptualizes and creates 3D character animation under the direction of the Lead Artist and Project Leader, meeting their quality, originality and creative standards. Entry-Level Salary Range: $54,600-$90,000.

Effects Animator

An Effects Animator renders natural and physical phenomena such as rain, fire and water to embellish the drawn or digital character's action in each scene. This Animator often works with various computer animation and effects programs to create these details. Entry-Level Salary Range: $40,000-$60,000.

Industrial Animator

The Industrial Animator usually works with corporations to help them create animated advertisements or presentations. Like other Animators, Industrial Animators create 2D and 3D images that show objects in motion or illustrate a process. These images convey or enhance an industrial (and opposed to entertainment) project's message. These skills may be applied at a company that needs pre-visualization of an object or machine. The Industrial Animator, for example, might animate a car engine to show how it works. Entry-Level Salary Range: $40,000-$65,000.

Still from *The End*, Alias|Wavefront

Real World Example
Clay Animator
JR Williams

About the Career/Typical Duties
Clay Animators create stop motion animation, developing figures by sculpting and shooting the animation frame by frame. We are pretty much expected to do a little of everything in addition to being the person on the set who is moving and sculpting the characters and operating the camera. There are also times when we design and build the characters from scratch, and occasionally we have to do a lot of sketching and drawing before we actually start the sculpting of a character. The same holds true with the sets.

A lot of times we will get an idea from an advertising agency that is representing clients of some kind, and sometimes the agency has come up with a concept or idea themselves, or they may come up with it working with their clients or whatever. Anyway, they can come to us with really well developed ideas and specific requests ready to go. But more often than not it comes to us rather vaguely and sometimes it is frequently up to us to generate character design ideas based on verbal descriptions we get from the agency people. There's a lot of hit and miss sometimes. We start out with a lot of sketches

Digital Artist at work, Waveworks Digital Media

incorporating their ideas and they'll choose elements and we'll go back and do more drawings.

There's also the story process during which they may send us a rough outline of what the commercial is about, what's going to happen in the commercial and what the story is. They might send us a storyboard either really quickly drawn or very lavishly drawn. It just depends on what we get from them.

We are also very active in all the design facets, all the storyboarding for our projects, and so there's a lot of give and take between the agency, the advertiser, and ourselves. It's almost always an extremely collaborative process between many different people, so there's never any single person or small group of people involved in the thing. It's almost always a pretty intense group effort. People have to be open to that. Anybody who's too sensitive about criticism about their own creativity is probably not going to last very long in this business because whatever project comes out of here is going to have an awful lot of ideas from very different people involved in it. Once we get past the design and storyboarding processes, we get into the animation part, and then things go a little more smoothly, but there are even instances where the animation isn't quite right the first, the second, or even the third time around; it has to be done over again. There have also been times when a commercial has been nearly completed and there's been something in the action that suddenly someone is not happy with and they want to make a change. It's sometimes really tough to do that but sometimes it's necessary.

So, it's definitely not a consistent process every time through. After I do the shot, it goes into the lab and comes back; I watch it with the Director, and then the Director comments and decides whether or not the shot is good enough or if it needs to be done again and the Director would sit down with the Animator on some type of equipment where they can load the film or video down and point out the things that he would like to change. If the work is fine then it's cut into the whole of the commercial or film or whatever it is you're making. And even then they may discover that there is a problem with continuity from one shot to the next, so something else might have to be changed. Even after your shot was approved, there can still be some changes that must be made.

Education

I do know that there are schools that have animation-based curriculum. Probably enrolling in something in that particular craft would be good. It doesn't hurt to have a background in other areas, because along with doing the animation and sculpting there is also work doing character and/or set design. I personally had a background in working with a lot of different materials, like Styrofoam, wood, working in a woodshop, doing a lot of painting, carving, real basic hands-on activities. Here at Vinton's there is an awful lot of emphasis placed on characterization in the animation, so any kind of theatrical background or even stage or film acting experience could be beneficial because you are actually making the characters act. So yes, I would say it could be beneficial in a lot of different ways.

Sources of Additional Information

If you're interested in learning about 3D Animation read *The Aardman Book of Filmmaking* by Peter Lord (Harry N Abrams; ISBN: 0810919966). You might also attend ASIFA meetings.

Real World Example
Forensics Animator
Rudy Mantel

About the Career/Typical Duties
As a Forensics Animator, I gather all the information required to understand what occurred, and I put that all together into an animation. I illustrate the story that our expert is trying to tell, what he said happened. You can show what happened from different angles or different views and then you have to decide which is the best view. You have no freedom in animating the event, or in what occurred, but you do have freedom in showing which views you're going to show and from which angles. You decide the best way to show what occurred.

I do animations to be shown in the courtroom or during mediation. It is a great mediation tool. In many cases, the exhibit never gets to the courtroom. It's used in mediation and clients' problems often get settled afterwards. It really helps obtain better results in mediation. I often work with engineers and with Accident Reconstructionists. It's a fairly new profession. They give me their information and I make a 3D animation sequence that is used as a courtroom exhibit. On an average day I spend a lot of time gathering information, seeing if I have a good drawings and the plans that I need. I often go out to the accident site myself to take photographs. Sometimes I even have to take measurements. But usually not. Usually the engineer gives me information. Then I sit down at my computer and I might spend a few days modeling the site and the vehicles. I spend another couple of days animating it, and then I might spend a couple of days editing it, putting it all together and making the titles. Then I send off a preliminary version to the lawyer and engineer, and then they say "well, you know, we really would have rather shown this from a different angle and I think we're going to change the speed." So then I have to do revisions and send that off. But I would say that I spend probably 80% of my time sitting at a computer. I use 3D Studio Max and that's my main computer program.

Education

I took a good many engineering courses when I was in college and I have a degree in Industrial Management from Georgia Tech. I would recommend engineering courses, courses in mathematics. You don't need anything very deep. I wouldn't go past Algebra and Trigonometry. I would say workers need engineering, mathematics, physics, computer and pencil drafting, and definitely 3D computer modeling and animation experience.

I spent most of my time as a professional pilot, and with that I got into accident investigation in aviation. Later I got interested in computer drafting which I learned just because I was interested. I took courses at a community college here in Florida, and then the modeling and animation software became available for the first time at an affordable cost that would run on a PC platform. The first software was 3D Studio Max and I taught myself how to use that. Forensics animation was just getting started then and I guess I was one of the early people in the field. It took a long, long time to get my name out there, and to get the first one or two jobs. Now I am quite well known and my business is quite good. But it took a long time because sometimes you have to testify in trials and they take your deposition. So you have to have a certain credibility and experience and it just takes a long time to work into that. To my knowledge there aren't any specific courses available in forensics animation, although there may be by now.

Salary

There is no such thing. I only know one Forensics Animator who isn't self employed. Most of us are hired by attorneys, often upon recommendation by an expert. We set our rates depending on the complexity and lengths of animation. We get a summary of what the accident is about and from that we can quote a price, but we're not really employed. I only know one guy who's permanently employed, full time, by an engineering company. Most of us are self-employed.

Sources of Additional Information
I would say there is something called the *Accident Recronstruction Journal* that may be useful. Certainly you should try and obtain a student version or copy of the software program that you will be using. *3D studio max* is a very popular one. You need a good computer too, with a fast graphics card, and a lot of memory, but those have come way down in price. Learn the software program and practice all you can. There are many books and tutorials out there.

Real World Example
3D Computer Animator
Dave Taylor-Audio Vision

About the Career/Typical Duties
3D Computer Animators use their artistry to create the nuances of motion, gesture and performance that bring characters to life. I do some effects, like video effects and transitional stuff like that, elements as far as background elements, and background shapes and logos, and that's about it. I do a lot of the production work.

Most of the animation requests come from corporate clients. They might need a logo or have graphics to add to a background. I utilize the phone a great deal. I usually load in the latest version of the project and build a wire frame. Maybe I get a really quick low resolution actual animation and take a look at it with all the textures and stuff like that built into it, and then see what I can do from there. Usually I get something rough down first, then move onto building the textures, and then adjust the lighting. I take off the generic lighting and see how things look with spotlights, shadows, etc. I probably work 50 to 60 hours a week.

Education

It is necessary to understand both traditional and newer methods of animation. 3D Animation requires the ability to draw, including an understanding color theory, life drawing, and composition. You must be able to use computer animation tools, and also electronic tools such as illustration, scanning and image manipulation tools. It's important to understand sketch ideas and storyboards.

Traditional animation training is highly valued. You need strong traditional skills, or experience with other media (cel, stop-motion, etc.) Experience with high-end animation software is preferred.

Salary

Entry level is around $20,000 or $30,000. It depends on the studio. I mean there are so many open fields for someone who knows animation. You can work in a corporate video realm, or get into game development, or you can get into some kind of Web application. It really depends where you end up in the company, and whether your company is going in a profitable direction. There's modeling of the objects, and then the animating of the object. Modeling, you can get by, because you can always buy objects already modeled. It's relatively cheap. For like $300 you can get yourself a fleet of aircrafts and can do animation with them. There are modeling houses too. When I was out there looking for models on the Web, I saw three or four postings for jobs. One was from a high-end, LA based post company. Another one was in Chicago. It kind of depends.

Real World Example
3D Computer Animator
Raquel Coelho

About the Career/Typical Duties
Well, basically we do a lot of commercials and short films. We have meetings with set motion. In my case, I do a little bit of story development too, developing the characters and all that stuff. So some Animators do that; some just do editing. When a project comes in the house, one of us goes out and does the character design or even the modelers do the character design. And sometimes we work with illustrators; we always have to talk to modelers and lighters. We do a lot of fun cartoon-type of animation; some of the commercials are really cool. They are short projects too. Often they are less tiring than a film because the film goes on for a year or two and you deal with the same characters all the time. In the commercial, we're doing the motions.

Education
I went to School of the Arts, Julliard. I did a Master's in Computer Art with concentration in Computer Animation. I have previous training in cel animation. I did a lot of 3D animation.

Salary
I would say something between $30,000 and $65,000 a year. I think Character Animators don't go much over, like about $150,000 something like that.

Sources of Additional Information
There is an International Association of Animators. They have a training program, animation competitions, and festivals. You could also get information from ASIFA.

Real World Example
Senior Animator
Doug Dooley

About the Career/Typical Duties
As a Senior Animator you use your artistry to create the
nuances of motion, gesture, and performance that bring
characters to life. I'm a senior Animator, which means that I
kind of overlook the setting up of the animation, making sure
that it's ready for Animators to go ahead and start moving
objects. I'll do a lot of the animation for commercials and movie
special effects. After I'm done working with a project, I hand it
off to a Technical Director who freezes it into our proprietary
software. I mean I'm actually the first person to start making
objects move. Then we have a team of Animators who will go
ahead and animate the entire commercial. When we're done, we
send our projects off to get lit.

Sometimes I just supervise a job, which means I won't animate
on it because I'll have another job but I'll be looking over
another job to make sure that the team of Animators on that job
aren't having any problems with things. I make sure that the rig
is set up the way it will be best for everyone, so I'll be working
on a couple of jobs that way. I'm also involved in setting
meetings, so when we get our commercial forwards in I'll try
and decide how long I think it'll take to do the animation. I also
decide which techniques would be best for a project, and
whether a project is practical for us to do. I also have been
leading up animation meetings. Actually, I have taken on a
couple, but we don't currently have a manager with our
animation department. I'm not a manager of the department,
but I've taken on a couple of duties where I'll set up animation
meetings, weekly animation meetings, so everyone can get to sit
down and discuss things if there's anything more they want to
discuss. I've been working on some reels, picking up demo reels,
to see if any of them are any good, even though we're not

hiring right now. There was a time when I was working with someone on a training program, or on animation exercises for people to do when things became slow and not all the Animators were busy.

I pretty much work 9:30 to 6:30, with an hour for lunch. I think it varies. The Technical Directors tend to have to work more hours. As the jobs come in people start getting behind in everything. We have to work more, extra hours. I've actually been pretty lucky where I usually don't have to. I usually get my stuff done pretty quickly.

I started just as a regular Animator here when the company was smaller. The role has changed so much that our jobs became more and more specialized. You know virtually, we started having a lead Animator for all of them, and people who were generally lead Animators became senior Animators. I guess just the experience of dealing with commercials as an Animator is crucial, to understand the rig process and what ways are best for setting up a character so that everyone can use it.

Education
Traditional animation training is highly valued. Have strong traditional skills or experience with other media (cel, stop-motion, etc.). Experience with high-end animation software and computer experience is preferred. Four years experience animating in a production environment is required.

Salary
It varies a lot. Most of the work is in LA, San Francisco, and New York. The salaries are roughly between $35,000 and $50,000.

Chapter 2
Modelers

Modeling is one of the stages in creating a 3D animation or a computer generated 3D animation. It is the stage that takes place after the storyboard is approved and the characters are designed on paper in a studio environment. The modeler in a studio environment must work closely with the agreed specifications for the models, working to duplicate the sketch in three dimensions. Some modelers work on marquette, others work to create models for clay animation, still others on the computer using software programs to create the digital model or wire frame model that will later be brought to life by the animation department. Modelers must have a keen sense of volume, geometry, and mass. This is true for all modelers, even the ones working on Computer Aided Design (CAD) or Computer Aided Manufacturing (CAM) or on computer generated three dimensional models like that of Toy Story. Today, several small animation companies purchase models rather than building them in houses. Companies such as Viewpoint Data Labs are staffed with modelers that build custom models.

From top to bottom: T-Rex wireframe model created by Viewpoint Data Labs; Clay model in progress, *A Little Curious* created by Curious Pictures for HBO.

Education

Modelers at animation studios often have an undergraduate degree in Fine Arts or Animation. Most have taken classes in ceramics, 3D design, and modeling. CAD modelers often have an undergraduate degree in Design or Engineering. Modelers often come from the Architecture field as well. Entry-Level Salary Range: $35,000-$100,000+.

Areas

3D Computer Modelers

These Modelers use three dimensional graphics software to build models on the computer via geometric structures. The Modeler builds characters and scenes in parts, and then assembles them together to make the final scene. The Modeler furnishes a final built character for the Animator who will bring the character to life in accordance with the script. Entry-Level Salary Range: $35,000-$60,000.

Model for HBO's *A Little Curious* by Curious Pictures

Modeler

On a live action film set the modeler may build and articulate geometric models, using plans, sketches and descriptions from the Art Director. This may include designing miniatures for a film project. Modelers work closely with the Art Director in the planning and construction stages of miniatures. The Modelers may sculpt objects from clay for a clay animation project or use a latex mold for stop-motion animation. Entry-Level Salary Range: $39,000-$109,000.

Real World Example
3D Computer Modeler
Alex Levinson, Blue Sky Studios

About the Career/Typical Duties
3D Computer Modelers build and articulate computer models, given plans, sketches, and descriptions from an Art Director

Day-to-day responsibilities include modeling on the computer any objects and characters that need to be modeled for commercials, animations, and/or films. Sometimes I get to do character design, usually on paper first. I'll sculpt from the paper design to get the finalized character shape and when the client approves those, I'll start building them on the computer. Let's say I have a wire frame on the computer at a place where I'm happy with it—it's time to start making the color surfaces textured, which we do via bump maps and color maps.

The Animators, the Modelers, the Technical Directors, we all work together because I'm going to build a model, and then it's going to go to an Animator and he/she's going to rig it. Then when the Animator is done rigging it, he's going to animate it and that same model now is in someone else's hands, and when he's done animating it, it's going to go to a Technical Director for lighting and rendering. So everyone's going to have his or her hands on that thing that I build. I want to make sure that everyone's clear what they're getting, and if anyone has any better ideas on what they would like to see, I can do it at the early stages.

Education

You need a blend of both technical and artistic skills. Have a good understanding of computer graphics, including the use of NURBS surfaces, Bezier or B-spline curves and surfaces, and subdivision surfaces. An ability to program in a variety of languages, including scripting languages (like Perl, TCL, AWK, or shell) and primary programming languages (like C or C++) is necessary, and also an understanding of linear algebra and basic matrix mathematics. Develop a sensitive eye for form and motion, and have good interpersonal skills. Be able to take directions (both art direction and technical advice) well. You need an understanding of GL or Open GL, and Renderman or MEL, and knowledge of APL or Matlab is a plus. Get UNIX and work on an SGI workstation using graphic packages (Alias, Maya, Wavefront, Softimage). Education can include Computer Science, Mathematics or Engineering, background or experience in art, which shows a thorough understanding of physical, motion, weight, balance, texture and form. Professional experience as a commercial artist is a plus.

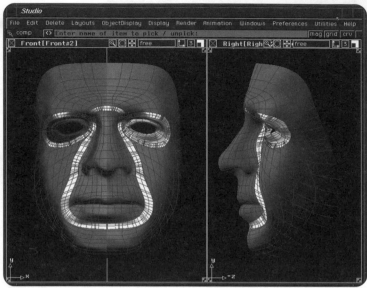

Facial model from *The End*, an animation created at Alias|Wavefront

I went to art school and I was majoring in illustration, with a minor in sculpture, and I had a classical background in painting and sculpture from that education. Anytime you use artistic tools, knowing art is important. A lot of people who I interview at Blue Sky come here with just computer experience, and once you manage the control over the computer, you are essentially an artist—you're no longer an art student. So education in art really plays a role in what kind of images you can make, and the bottom line in this field is image-making ability.

Chapter 3
Designers

A designer is a person trained to solve a functional physical problem by communicating visually. Designers must rely on their own artistic facilities for graphic and aesthetic design. They must keep in mind concerns of lighting, spacing, color, texture, size, etc.

Responsibilities

Whether in type and image, on screen or on signs, the fundamental principles for design are the same. The tools are often the same but methodologies are not. Web design is not the same as graphic design, and graphic design is not the same as character design. A designer may specialize in various forms of design as a means of increasing volume of work.

Environmental shot of R/GA Studio

The responsibilities of Junior Designers vary from firm to firm. A Junior Designer at a design firm usually assists various projects, from the creation of annual reports, to the creation of brochures and Web pages. On the other hand, a Junior Designer at any in-house corporate or business art/ design department is often given a single task. While it is important to build expertise in whatever field you are in, it is always consequential to expand your knowledge base.

All Designers must keep up with the changes in the tools of the trade and the various techniques being introduced. Experienced designers must confirm to broaden their range of expertise to the digital areas.

Education

From the onset a designer's education is very interdisciplinary. It is important that they learn as much as possible about the various areas of design before securing a niche. Most junior designers are often required to do various kinds of designing at a general design firm.

A Bachelor's degree in fine art, graphic design, or visual communications is helpful. Designers, like most artists, demonstrate their abilities via a portfolio of their work rather than a resume. To get the skills necessary to assemble such a portfolio, most entry-level portfolios include a large percentage of school assignments, and often one or two redesigns of existing magazines. This shows the artist's ability to solve design problems. Typography and layout samples should also be prepared at college. Learn the techniques of the trade: how to layout, illustrate, and work with font on the Graphic Designer's computer of choice... The Macintosh.

Entry-Level Salary Range:$35,000-$100,000+.

Areas

Graphic Designer

The Graphic Designer uses visual media to convey a message. Graphic Designers tend to use computers almost exclusively for designing, sketching, and manipulating images. Many Graphic Designers perform a broad range of tasks, switching from one medium to another at their clients' demands. Graphic Designers may work in various industries, including newspapers, book publishing, music recording, and advertising. Graphic Designers work with several computer software programs for the purpose of designing graphics for print media. Graphics Designers are interested in framing ideas, projecting attitudes, promulgating styles, and managing information. The impulse to become a Graphic Designer is not exclusive to those in the applied or fine arts. Anyone interested in "visuals" is a prospective candidate. People engaged in graphic design—in-house or staff designers, freelancers, and principals of independent firms—all need some shared fundamental knowledge. Graphic Designers may specialize in a number of fields including television, film, computer graphics, set design, corporate design, book and magazine design, advertising, and illustration. They may progress to positions including Design Director, Art Director, and/or Creative Director. Entry-Level Salary Range: $16,000-$60,000.

Senior Graphics Designer

The senior designer is responsible for conceptualization and design of solutions from concept to completion. At some firms, a senior designer may direct the work of one or more Junior Designers, who generate comps (composites are also called roughs or mockups of the end product) and create layouts and final art. In some cases, Senior Designers do not manage a staff but are designated "senior" because of their authority in design decision-making. Entry-Level Salary Range: $50,000-$70,000.

Environmental Graphic Designer

Environmental Designers are concerned with the look and feel of signs, which might include anything from a simple retail shop shingle to an entire directional system for a hospital, theater or museum. The Environmental Designer is responsible for the information and design. Environmental Designers often work in a group with other Graphic Designers to devise systems that are easy to follow and aesthetically pleasing within the environment. Entry-Level Salary Range: $35,000- $55,000.

Promotion Designer

The Promotion Designer works for a specific company and designs the material necessary to sell the company services or products. The Promotion Designer's output may include brochures, slide presentations, catalogues, posters, and mailings. The Promotion Designer assigns work to freelance photographers and illustrators, and must establish and maintain satisfactory working relationships with many others. Promotion Designers need to be able to design, layout, and sketch projects. They must know how to use type and color well, and be thoroughly familiar with production methods and reproduction techniques. Entry-Level Salary Range: $30,000-$50,000.

Municipal Graphic Designer (Urban Planning Designer)

The Municipal Graphic Designer designs signs and symbols for a city in order to make travel directions clearly understood, even to people unfamiliar with the city and its language. The work of a Municipal Graphic Designer appears in parks, municipal buildings, on city vehicles, subway systems and in bus stations. Entry-Level Salary Range: $30,000-$45,000.

Record Cover Designer

This designer does the graphic design of record album covers, creating a visual counterpart to the musical mood of an album. A design decision is arrived at with the input of the record company sales department, and with respect to the wishes of the featured recording artist. If the Designer decides to work from a photograph of the musical artist, the Designer may choose to work with the photography studio to determine the look, lighting, and mood of the photograph. Record Cover Designers must be aware of the current musical trends. A successful cover has the right balance of photography, color, and fonts. Entry-Level Salary Range: $30,000-$45,000.

Book Designer

The Book Designer often receives credit under the title of Layout Design as he or she is chiefly concerned with the inside pages, the guts of the book. This Designer has expertise in typography. Book design requires the ability to transfer a typewritten manuscript into a typeset book. Knowledge of bookbinding is helpful. The job requires highly refined judgment with the ability to balance type and illustration on a page in order to produce the most effective publication possible. Entry-Level Salary Range: $30,000-$45,000.

Book Jacket Designer

Book Jacket Designers create the cover design for books. This Artist may be employed by a design studio specializing in book jacket design, or may work on a freelance basis. The purpose of a book jacket design is to promote the sale of the book, using type either alone or in conjunction with photography and/or illustration. The Book Jacket Designer has a strong sense of design and knowledge of the latest developments in typography. The Designer assigns work to Photographers and Illustrators. Entry-Level Salary Range: $30,000-$45,000.

Information Designer

An Information Designer is mainly concerned with the presentation of text information. The role of the Information Designer is to guide users away from confusion into understanding, regardless of subject. The focus is not on style and flair but rather function and utility of the information to accomplish clear communication. This Designer often employs the use of facts, figures and charts. Information Designers are in various proportions typographers, statistical analysts, mapmakers, and reporters. They must constantly draw upon their instincts in these areas to make design decisions. Entry-Level Salary Range: $30,000-$45,000.

Desktop Publisher

The Desktop Publisher designs and creates documents, brochures, and publications using page layout software. The text, images, and other information are supplied to the Desktop Publisher who chooses the fonts and layout. The term Desktop Publisher covers a variety of professionals who design and create documents ranging from simple reports or brochures to page layouts for magazines and books. Entry-Level Salary Range: $30,000-$45,000.

Concept art, *A Little Curious* created by Curious Pictures for HBO.

Character Designer

The Character Designer creates the visual depiction of the character to be used in an animation or film. The Character Designer is an Illustrator who creates the portrayal of the characters. Before an animation can be created, a script must be written. The script introduces a cast of fictional characters. It is the Character Designer's job to read the script and determine or propose what these characters will look like. These characters are then used in the storyboard. Character Designers almost always work part-time or as freelance illustrators. At smaller companies, the Character Designer may also layout the storyboards, and do general design work. Entry-Level Salary Range: $35,000-$60,000.

Industrial Designer (Product Designer)

Industrial Designers create and produce designs for commercial, medical, and industrial products. They make models and prototypes of these designs for mass production. Their products cover a wide range of manufactured goods from toys and toasters, to furniture, and heavy machinery. While some work is carried out on the development of new products, other work is related to updating and improving the design of existing products. Industrial Designers discuss manufacturers' and clients' requirements. They undertake research and development, and consider factors influencing product design such as cost and availability of materials. They prepare presentations about their projects, and supervise construction of models. Finally, they test their products' functionality, quality, and consumer appeal. Entry-Level Salary Range: $30,000-$50,000.

Designer at the R/GA's design studio

Instructional Designer

Instructional Designers create and revise learning support resources and delivery/assessment methodologies. Instructional Designers increasingly use the flexibility offered by multimedia applications to target specific learning objectives and audiences. The incorporation of multimedia technologies in instructional design work can provide the combined benefits of interactivity, and realistic audio and video. Instructional Designers develop effective and innovative design strategies, applying audio, animations, graphics, text, motion video, and photos to clearly illustrate specific ideas. Use a variety of software programs, formatted templates and production pathways. Entry-Level Salary Range: $26,000-$50,000.

Web Designer

Web Designers create Web pages that contain information in the form of text and graphics. They start with information or data to be published on the World Wide Web. The Web Designer is responsible for presenting this information through the use of text, multiple pages, and links. The Web Designer must first work with clients to understand the information that needs to be presented on the Web page. The Web Designer then storyboards the information so that the client understands and approves the project. Next, the designer locates images and graphics that will be used on the Web page. This often involves manipulating existing graphics, optimizing and resizing graphics, and laying out graphics so that text and images are in harmony. Once layout is complete the designer creates links and buttons to navigate the new Web pages. Web designing is a fusion of layout, design, typography, graphic design, book design, and basic programming in HTML. Entry-Level Salary Range: $20,000-$70,000 (average salary of approximately $40,000) Freelance Web Designers can make as much as $50,000 designing a major corporate Web page.

Webmaster

The Webmaster maintains and often creates sites for the World Wide Web. He or she provides content and updates the site on a regular basis. The Webmaster monitors the performance and popularity of the site and often is the one who registers the site with search engines. The Webmaster is also the first point of contact if visitors to the site require technical assistance. A Webmaster may oversee several sites at a time as a freelancer. He or she may also be on staff as a Webmaster for a popular site that receives thousands of hits (visitors) per month. For some Webmasters, patrolling and updating dead links means full time employment. Entry-Level Salary Range: $35,000-50,000.

IBM.com Web design project created by R/GA for IBM

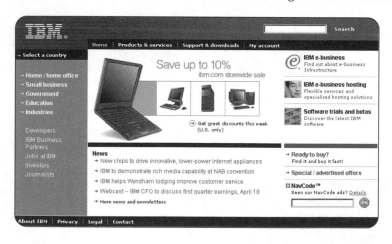

RISD.com Web design project created by R/GA for Rhode Island School of Design;

Multimedia Developer

Multimedia Developers generate and manipulate graphic images, animations, sound, text, and video into consolidated and seamless multimedia programs. Multimedia applications include computer-based training programs, data presentation programs, CD-ROMs, entertainment programs, and educational programs. Multimedia Developers consult with clients to determine project requirements. They analyze and recommend appropriate software platforms to achieve their clients' objectives, and create flow diagrams and storyboards to outline their creative concept. They prepare 2D and 3D animations, video/sound clips, and graphic images. They retouch and manipulate images and concepts, and manage the development and implementation of multimedia products. Entry-Level Salary Range: $27,000-$40,000.

Prop Designer

A Prop Designer creates various objects for use on a movie or television set. The Prop Designer works with the Stylist and others, such as the Prop Master, to dress the set and match the Art Director's vision. The Prop Designer brings into existence all of the special items in a shot. They might, for example, create a

Designer at the R/GA's design studio

newspaper with a fake headline. Entry-Level Salary Range: starting salary-$25,000- $35,000.

Production Designer

The Production Designer develops a visual plan for an entire production, including sets, props, costumes, color schemes, and lighting schemes. He/she makes a thorough study of the script, does research, and confers with the Producer and Director to develop the "look" and flow of a film from one sequence to the next. Entry-Level Salary Range: $35,000-$40,000.

Assistant Game Designer

Game Designer studios work on the development of video or CD-ROM games often for outside clients. These games can be educational or purely for entertainment. The Assistant Game Designer is expected to contribute to the initial game planning through scripting and game balancing. Entry-Level Salary Range: $25,000-$50,000.

Game Designer

The Game Designer is responsible for conceptualizing all elements of the game design, taking a game project from its initial vision, through research, concept, and on-going design, eventually bringing the project to a successful completion. The Game Designer usually provides leadership in the visual design of a game and in the programming necessary for execution. He/she must be thorough, and must be able to prevent design drift by enforcing his or her vision. Game Designers are often required to have a strong display of academic credentials. Employers look for strong written and verbal communication skills and a good understanding of graphics implementation. Game Designers also need experience designing AI, and an ability to identify and develop core fun elements in a game's design. Entry-Level Salary Range: $50,000-$75,000+.

Image of *Jeopardy*, Web design created by R/GA for Sony

Lead Game Designer

A game studio is often broken up into small groups. Each group has a Lead Designer and various other practitioners that work on the components of the game. The Lead Designer provides direction to other designers on the team. He or she supervises the visual and design, and above all, communicates the game concept to the team. This individual creates and writes the original Game Concept Documents, including the Core and Essence Statements, Game Mechanics Documents (how the game works in terms of the game world including things like movement, combat and the workings of the AI) and Creative Design Documents (characters, background, game play, world structure). Lead Designer creates and writes the game Technical Specifications (detailed listing of game feature, interface option and to some degree, game variables). Further, the Lead Game Designer creates and writes game fiction as necessary including plot, storyline, voice scripting, data scripting, and more. The Lead Designer is also skilled in game balance issues, such as combat resolution formulas, character statistics, and object properties, etc. Entry-Level Salary Range: $75,000+.

Architect

An Architect designs buildings, consulting with engineers to design sound structures. They negotiate with builders and planning authorities, administer building contracts and inspect the work carried out. Architects discuss requirements of clients or builders (to design a new structure or modify an existing one), prepare detailed drawings, and make presentations about their project plans. Their planning can be undertaken by hand or by utilizing computer-aided design (CAD) equipment. Their work combines structural, mechanical, and artistic elements. They discuss designs and cost estimates with clients and others involved in the project, including engineers, quantity surveyors, landscape Architects, and town planners. They obtain necessary approvals from local authorities, and prepare contract documents specifying building materials, construction equipment, and, in some cases, interior furnishings. The Architect's plans are utilized by builders, trades people, and legal advisers. The Architect observes, inspects, and monitors building work to ensure that it is progressing according to the contract specifications. When the workers are finished and the building is standing, the Architect conducts post occupancy evaluations to ensure that all work is up to standards. Architects may also be involved in project feasibility studies, strategic asset investigations and heritage studies. Architects often specialize in particular types of work, for example, domestic, low-rise commercial, high-rise commercial, industrial, conservation and heritage buildings. Architects need to keep up with changing trends in the construction industry and the community. They have considerable contact with the public. Entry-Level Salary Range: $25,000-$55,000.

Set Designer

Set Designers draft the necessary drawings that serve as guidelines for the production of a movie or theater stage. In order to design and create stage sets, the Set Designer must have knowledge of illustration, drafting, painting, model building, carpentry, and lighting. Ideas must be articulated in

sketches and models clearly enough so that Producers, Directors, Costume Designers, Lighting Designers and Carpenters can understand them. The Set Designer also supervises the actual construction of sets. Entry-Level Salary Range: $25,000-$50,000.

Interior Design by JMGR Architecture Engineering

Interior Designer

Interior Designers supervise the construction or redevelopment of building interiors to suit the needs of inhabitants. Interior Designers consult with clients and Architects to work out client needs and intentions. Based on their clients needs, they prepare drawing and specifications for interior construction. They ensure safety requirements and aesthetic appeal. They estimate costs, and submit estimates to clients for approval. They also supply detailed instructions to trades people, inspect the work of trades people, maintain scheduling and quality control, and collaborate with specialists in technical areas concerned with fire, hydraulics, electrics, and structural design. Interior Designers may also prepare exhibitions, commercial display stands, and TV/film production sets. Entry-Level Salary Range: $30,000-$50,000.

Environmental Designer

The Environmental Designer is a blend of the Interior Designer and Architect positions. Environmental Designers are concerned with the aesthetics of building environments from the exterior to the interior. Kurt Shade explains, "You are looking at the environment holistically, as opposed to say an Architect who may deal with more specific things in terms of door jams, etc."

Audio Designer

Audio Designers create a coherent and consistent sound design for the communications of their clients. They ensure the production and postproduction of music, voice, and effects. They are responsible for creating sound that is useful and desirable to their clients. Audio Designers create audio (music, sound effects, voice) for all digital platforms. They research and develop audio systems that will better serve their current task, and they work closely with other team members to ensure that the audio delivered is in accordance with the vision of their client. They set the tone/style/voice of the audio. Audio Designers define the amount of time and effort it will take to finalize audio based on the needs of the client. They also edit and arrange existing audio. Sometimes a client may already own existing audio clips including voiceovers, speeches, mnemonics, and songs. In this case the job will be to appropriately make use of these for the purpose of the current project. The Audio Designer may also mix and manipulate sound or design sound to picture. Audio Designers must have an understanding of songwriting and arrangement principles. Entry-Level Salary Range: $30,000-$45,000.

User Interface Designer

The User Interface Designer designs the program interface, the buttons and icons that open and control programs within the computer. Interface designers create the appearance and function of the computer's interactive capabilities. The Interface Designer is chiefly concerned with creating a user-friendly software program. They design all interactive elements, including menu bars and screen buttons. They decide upon the placement of all interactive buttons on the screen, and choose foreground and background colors for screen imagery. Entry-Level Salary Range: $40,000- $60,000.

Real World Example
Graphic Designer
Rick Heffner

About the Career/Typical Duties
A Graphic Designer is someone who combines visual and verbal messages into one unified message, someone who takes all the ingredients and makes certain the final execution is a well-balanced piece of art, one message. The primary consideration is design, but Graphic Designers also have contact with clients and vendors, so good communication skills are necessary.

This job can be stressful; people here manage anywhere from 5-10 projects at one time. The job entails some design, a lot of phone time, dealing with clients. The job is rewarding and usually everyone's happy at the end of the day.

Education
I was very involved in my high school art department, and in college I did the same thing. I worked in the field. You definitely need some kind of college background. I majored in Graphics Design. Art programs alone are not going to get you where you need to be. You have to have a well-balanced and rounded career or education. You need to know your literature and have your sciences, because they are all going to come into play at some point. Liberal arts schools will probably be best. A Fine Arts background is definitely important!!

Salary
Entry is probably in the high $20,000's. It depends on the number of years. It's kind of hard to say. The high end is probably $60,000+.

Sources of Additional Information
If you're interested in the field you could join AIGA- the American Institution of Graphics Arts. It's a national organization with chapters in each major city. You might also try the Art Directors Club of DC. We have a local chapter. Read Communications Arts publications, like How Magazine, and Print Magazine.

Real World Example
Environmental Designer
Kurt Shade

About the Career/Typical Duties
Take an Interior Designer and an Architect, and mash their jobs together—that's what an Environmental Designer is. You are looking at the environment holistically, as opposed to say an Architect who may deal with more specific things in terms of door jams, etc. You look at it in its totality, in terms of what is the first impression we want people to get of the space, of the store, of the environment. It's more from a visual level than from an Architectural level. It's considered environmental because it impacts from the exterior to the interior, as opposed to where most Architects are concerned with the exterior and the shell, and then you have Interior Designers who are more focused on the interior. We're focused all the way through from exterior to the interior. Because of our designs, we impact all of that. The clients tell us the way they want their store to look, and we tell them how we think the name should be presented. We impact the overall environment.

The job responsibilities vary from project to project, and from day to day. It depends on what stage you are in on a project. Some projects have been developed, and some projects are just getting started. So if a project hasn't been developed, there is a certain amount of research that's involved in terms of what the client's business is, how they operate, and how their supplies are stocked and replenished. You also need to research what the building and environment look like at the present time. If a building doesn't exist yet, you can research styles of similar business offices. Then there usually comes a time when you are just generating ideas about all kinds of things, like exteriors, furnishings, and fixtures. It depends on what stage of the project we are in. The project stage really determines what I'm doing on a day-to-day basis. Sometimes I'm juggling several projects at a time (maybe two, three, four projects). So, each of them will be at different stages.

Education

I attended the Institute of Design and Construction in New York (DCNY). Then I went to the New York Institute of Technology (NYIT). I attended the Associates program at DCNY, and then I went to NYIT for their four-year Architecture program.

My education was unique in the fact that I did Architecture and Interior Design in the Industrial Design department. I think it exposed me more to the whole holistic approach in terms of going from the exterior inwards, then looking at the function and spatial requirements. I think it gave me a well-rounded approach to looking at the whole picture, as it relates to design. Being able to visualize things in your mind's eye and then to kind of put them on paper is extremely important. I can't say I can pinpoint one particular thing, because all those things impacted me in helping me to be able to do the things I do.

There isn't really a true Environmental Design training program, because you could come at it from several directions. You can come at it from Architecture, or you can come from interior design. It's just a matter of supplementing what the formal educational training leaves out. You will add to your training while you're on the job. It's good to take a lot of the history and drawing classes. The drawing ones are especially useful, in order to see things in 3Dimensions, to see them before you even put pen to paper to develop your sight in terms of how you look at things.

A Bachelors Degree would be sufficient to get you started. A Master's helps you to go to a greater depth in whatever else you are doing. But I think a Bachelor's is enough to get you started. Studying perspective drawing, history of Architecture, history of Design, or any of the Architectural design courses is very useful to this job.

Salary
Entry could be probably in the mid $20,000 range. The advanced salary depends on many factors. There are certain people at certain high levels that are almost at the point where they just do a couple quick sketches and then hand them off. Those high ups are probably at the $120,000 level. But they are few and far in between.

Real World Example
Freelance Character Designer
Greg Dyer

About the Career/Typical Duties
A Freelance Character Designer is a person who takes the concept of the character and brings it to fruition, who creates the visual depiction of the character. When I develop a character I work out the proportions of it. I create a front view, profiles, a backside, etc. so that people can see what the character looks like in a turn around view. When the Animators get it they need to know what the proportions of it are. I give them the angles that they'll be drawing everything from. Sometimes I'll do some concept drawings, maybe almost like key frame animations to show some of the range of motion the characters have. I do a

lot of 3D modeling too. Sometimes I even do a few simple animations to show what the characters can do.

If I'm doing a character job, somebody (a client) will give me a concept of a character. I'll talk to him or her a few times on the phone. I'll ask a whole lot of questions, like what the character is and what it does. Then I do some preliminary sketches (maybe three,) and I'll usually just email those sketches to the client. Then I'll get the client's' comments on the sketches, and I'll go back and do one more revision before I do the final product. I send a finished draft to them, and they'll look at it and tell me if there are any other changes. If I were going to do a 3D model of it too I would do a turn around drawing, including a side view, front view, and rear view. I'll then build the character and take another look before I start doing textures and stuff.

Education

I would recommend that a student going into fine arts get a BFA. Doing life drawings helps a lot, and so does knowing anatomy. Look at a lot of things like comics, and watch a lot of animations.

Salary

It depends on where you're at. It varies. But they pay pretty well at starting out. If you do really well and get connected, you can get paid very well. You really do a lot of things. If you're working on video games or something, you could do some modeling, 3D, and character design of your character. I think they start anywhere from $45,000-$60,000. From there it depends on your skills.

Sources of Additional Information

Join SIGGRAPH or E3. Also look into arts publications. There are a lot of publications if you're doing the 3D work, like modeling and animation references, and different magazines like *3D Design*. Read Disney's book *The Illusion of Life* (Hyperion; ISBN: 0786860707).

Real World Example
Print Advertiser
Robert Bowen

About the Career/Typical Duties
Basically we do custom visual effects for print advertising. We do a lot of very big ad campaigns. Lots of times, advertising agencies outsource campaigns to artists and I'm fortunate to be able to pitch and bid on a lot of those jobs. What we do is we sort of work in a team with a Photographer and an Art Director. We're in charge of the computer side.

Education
I studied film and video and then I edited a book about art and science. Then I got interested in computer graphics quite a bit, sort of a new field. I met a bunch of computer artists and then decided to get seriously involved in that, so I went back to school for a semester, studying computer science. I don't think there was any computer graphics course at the time. I studied programming, and then I came out and I got a job working as an Animator in a computer graphics company. We did a lot of television commercials. I worked at that for many years and then ended up going to another place where I worked on feature films, and also some TV. After that, I started my own company.

Sources of Additional Information
Get information from SIGGRAPH.

Real World Example
Web Designer
Michael Schreiber

About the Career/Typical Duties
A Web Designer is someone who creates and manages content
and design of Web pages. Web Designers also oversee interface
design. As a designer my primary responsibility is page design,
making sure a page is functional and attractive. On a usual
design day, I come in, gather work, sketch ideas, talk with the
Art Director, get some input, and do art in Photoshop or
Illustrator. When I'm finished working I tweak things, put
everything onto the Web page, and start fine-tuning.

Education
Mostly, I did a lot of research and training. I got a lot of highly
recommended books and took some courses that were available.
A college-based education is important, especially on the
programming side of the design. If you want to do really well,
just find a designer and do an internship with them, because
they are really going to be able to teach you everything that
you're going to need to know. Having a fine arts background is
important but not necessary. Qualified people have 2-3 years
Web experience and formal design training with strong
typographical, motion graphic, and interaction design skills. An
in-depth understanding of HTML and Web browsers is essential,
and knowledge of Photoshop and Illustrator is required (Flash is
a plus.) As for technical background and experience, some
programming knowledge is good also. I did get a break though
from working at AT&T for a while. So programming experience,
and some previous work design that you did are important to
your portfolio and resume.

Salary
Beginning salary could range from $30,000 to $45000. It
depends on where: New York, Omaha, or Nebraska. In New

York, for a designer, I would say between $40,000 to $50,000 is a good to start. If the designer is using JAVA, which is a demanding language, I would say $60,000.

Sources of Additional Information
There are a lot of really good Websites. Webmonkey.com is one. Depending on how much programming you want to get into, there are a lot of dynamic HTML sites. Usually you just search around on the net for your interests. You can pretty much find a good site for everything. In terms of design, there are a lot of good design books out there.

Real World Example
Game Designer
Sonya Shannon

About the Career/Typical Duties
The Game Designer is responsible for conceptualizing all elements of the game design. I'm working at a small startup company who's developing an engine. I really grew up with this technology. I've been very involved in the dialogue between artists and programmers, and am hoping to open that dialogue even more so artistic people will be drawn to using the computer. I do it all, from writing a manual on how to use the tools and software, to conceiving and doing all the creative work on a game. I help write the Game Bible, which is the document that explains all the rules of the game, who the character are, what's going to happen on each level, and what the back story is. I also get the models that I want. These are the human models to pose as the different characters. They act out different ranges of expression using physical gestures. I direct the motion cast when we get to that stage. Right now we're at the stage of designing the characters, designing their range of movement and building the geometry. I'm pretty much heading up that whole process and I have people working under me.

I find myself working about eight, then, or twelve hours a day, about five days a week. I'm not doing six and seven days a week right now, but when I began production it was really difficult. I was working six and seven days each week for very long hours. It was difficult because when we were under deadline, we worked 14 to 16 hours a day.

Education

I went to school at Sheraton College in Canada. I started my career as a computer Animator in 1982.

Salary

Well, salary depends very much on talent and level of command. For example, I can think of a student who was extremely talented. She was sought after by about thirteen companies. She had worked in the electronic theater, SIGGRAPH, and she started at $60,000 a year. That's about the highest that I've ever heard coming out of school, and this is out of a graduate program. She had already had a career as an illustrator before going to graduate school, and that was really at a very booming time for the industry.

Right now it's a little bit in the slump. It goes up, it kind of goes in cycles, but I would say more typically, people start at $35,000 or $40,000 if they're not that outstandingly talented. And it depends on the house too. Well, I have one friend on the West Coast who started before I did, he started in about '77, '78, '79, somewhere in the late 70s, and he's been making over $200,000 a year. Now this is somebody who could do anything and solve any kind of problem that you throw at him, so that's a highly desirable position to be in. Not many people can get there even after 10 years. I would say that physically if you're really great and you're looking on the West Coast, maybe $120,000 for a fairly senior person, $150,000 for somebody who's really extraordinary, but the average person I think would still be more likely $80,000 or $90,000.

Real World Example
Architect
Jayraj Raval, JMGR Architecture Engineering

About the Career/Typical Duties
I consider myself an Architect. I'm a person who builds environments. If you come to me as a client, and want my services, there's a good chance that you can ask me to design everything you're looking for because I know more about how an environment should be. So it's very environment oriented, and I think we need to all be designing environments instead of Architecture. I don't think there really is a profession called Architecture any longer, so it's really surroundings. That's all we do. That's what Architects do nowadays.

I'm an Architect Intern and basically I work underneath a Project Manager who is very much involved with how everything is done. I answer a lot of his questions and help him. He doesn't sit down and figure out all the detail work. Rather, I do all the detail work, and most of the CAD work. After about a year of interning you are considered Intermediate, and then you become licensed, and take a licensing exam that is really nine-exams-in-one. You have to pass all those nine exams to be professionally qualified, and after you do that, you basically specialize in a certain kind of field and hopefully stick with it. An average day is really different for a lot of people. Usually, we come in and follow up on our emails. After we get our emails answered, we usually work on assigned projects. Everybody is assigned a project and we all have to meet our own deadlines. It's very project oriented and everybody tackles their own projects in a given set period because everyone wants to meet deadlines and meet budgets.

Usually projects go through three stages. The first phase is called schematic design. The second phase is called design development. The third is called construction documentation. The first phase is all single line drawings. During the second phase we start putting thickness in the walls, making windows look like real windows. In the construction documentation phase we are basically putting in notes, dimensions, and stuff like that.

Education
I got a Bachelors of Architecture. I recommend taking classes like Auto CAD, and Photoshop—all the software that is out there that makes this profession a lot easier. There is tons of it out there, but just being computer oriented helps because most of the plans and everything are digital now. We usually send people CDs instead of final drawings on paper. Anything that has to do with computers is really good. I definitely recommend a student getting a degree first before becoming an Architect, always.

Fine Arts and historical knowledge are also very important for design, because everything nowadays is very materialistic, unlike in the old days. People right now want funky stuff in their living areas. Living areas are not meant to last a hundred years like they used to last in history. Now people build buildings that cost billions of dollars, but after 10 years they're tearing them down.

There's not any mathematics involved in Architecture. Architects need to be familiar with all the products and material that people build with, and that knowledge is something we don't get in school. We learn here in the industry.

Salary
It varies from state to state. In Tennessee it's like $25,000+ as soon as you enter the field and then when you reach three

years, which is Intermediate level, it jumps up to $37,000 or $38,000. Five to seven years after you get your license salary jumps up to $50,000 or $55,000.

Sources of Additional Information
There are a lot of conferences and organizations like AIA (American Institute of Architects). All of the organizations related to Architecture are on the Internet, and they all have Websites. Even all the manufacturers have Websites. When we're trying to pull a lot of resource material out, we jump on the Internet. The Internet has revolutionized the way we work in our office.

Some magazines that are good are *Catalyst,* and *Cadence.* There's an Auto CAD magazine that is good called *CAD Master.* As far as books, there are a ton of books out, like 3D Max and Auto CAD books, which you can find at bookstores. But a lot of it is on the Internet. You can get a lot of questions answered if you go on the news group servers.

Chapter 4
Creative and Technical Directors

The Director is the manager of the creative team. A successful project, whether feature film or computer animation, is contingent on the ability of the Director to work with various practitioners to realize his or her vision. Director's roles may vary depending on the medium.

Directors usually report to the producers of a project, collaborating with the producers to create their quality projects.

Responsibilities

The Director must oversee all the creative components of the project. The Director on a film must approve (often along with others) the actor, the set, the lighting, scripting, and all other production elements. He or she must work with the Producer and Art Director to agree upon a budget. Directors are the chief critics of the aesthetics of a project. They often suggest creative members of the production team to the Producers. They may hire and/or fire members of the production team.

In Animation, the Director reviews the progress of the animation team daily. The Director recommends voice talents, works with the Technical Directors to determine the tools necessary for the project, and works with the Character Designer and Storyboard Artist to approve the camera angles. The Director also reviews the work of the modeling, lighting, and postproduction departments.

Still from Alias|Wavefront's *Bingo* created by Chris Landreth

Education

All creative leaders should have an understanding of fine art, communication theory, composition, and color theory. In addition, print-based Art Directors should understand type and typography, design concept, and the technological and traditional tools of the trade. In addition to the general requirements of creative leaders, Art Directors should be diverse. They need to understand every angle of the production. Because Directors need to develop the ability to communicate visually it is important for them to spend the time developing these skills at a University or Art College. Print-based Directors should have a Bachelor of Arts degree in Visual Communications or Graphics Design from a well-structured design department.

Animation Directors likewise must spend the time to create an independent animation and some group projects where they are given the opportunity to direct a creative team. A four-year degree in animation will give them the time to develop an animation demo reel. The demo reel demonstrates the individual's ability to understand the different areas of the production and their ability to direct the camera in an animation.

The film/video area has similar requirements. They must take the initiative to create a short independent film during their college career. They must acquire the skills necessary for directing the camera. The demo reel must contain a well thought out and executed short project. Their ability to work with a creative production team is also important, so therefore besides the independent film, they should have worked with a group to help create or preferably direct films/videos. A BA or BFA. in Film/Video Production with the right mix of theory and practice is paramount.

Entry-Level Salary Range

Entry-Level Salary $30,000-$100,000+ depending on the medium and location. Creative Directors or Art Directors for print are more likely to be on the lower end of this scale, whereas Feature Film Directors can go way beyond this scale into the millions.

Areas

Creative Director of Animation (Computer)

The Creative Director of Animation oversees the creation of storyboards and the actual production of animation sequences. He or she makes sure that the animation team is on the right track in terms of concept, design, and work schedule. The Creative Director of Animation works with a team of Animators and production specialists, such as modelers and lighting people, to communicate his/her vision for the project. At large studios, the Creative Director works with the Director of Animation and Animation Supervisors, rather than with the specialists themselves. Entry-Level Salary Range: $50,000-$200,000.

Director of Animation (Cel)

The Director of Animation works with the story department on ideas, supervises the development of the stories, approves character sketches, directs recording of dialogue and music, creates the bar sheets, works with the layout person, delegates work to the Animators, supervises the pencil test and orders retakes, oversees the painting of the backgrounds, checks the rushes, and okays the final photography and the answer print. The Director also has the power to suggest hiring and firing to the Producer. Entry-Level Salary Range: $47,000-$63,000.

Art Director

The Art Director is the creative liaison between the client and technicians on a design or art project. The Art Director often meets directly with the client, to deduce what the client's needs are, to come up with several solutions and proposals for those needs. With the client's approval of a proposed concept, the Art Director begins working with Artists and Technicians to bring the concept to video, film, or print. The Art Director has managerial duties, interpersonal skills, and a good sense of time and scheduling because there is a lot that involves just basic management. He or she must have the ability to work well under pressure. Individual Producers who sell their products to networks employ many Art Directors, who commonly work on a freelance basis for producers of films, ad agencies, design firms or publishing companies. Entry-Level Salary Range: $30,000-$55,000.

Director of Postproduction

The Director of Postproduction coordinates, organizes, and manages the activities of the postproduction process required to complete a feature film, television program, or commercial. He/she makes decisions on the allocation of work and is responsible for making sure dailies are completed and delivered to appropriate places. The Director of Postproduction makes certain the postproduction process for a particular picture is operating within budget. Entry-Level Salary Range: $50,000-$75,000.

Creative Director (Web)

The Creative Director is responsible for designing the look of the Website, overseeing the creative development of the color, form and function of the site. The Creative Director works on a team with the Web Designer, Web Developer, Contract Producer and Producer, but is known as the driving creative force of the project. The Creative Director works closely with this team to

ensure that the aesthetic goals are accomplished. Entry-Level
Salary Range: $50,00-$80,800.

Director of Tools (Interactive)

The Director of Tools is responsible for managing the delivery of
system tools products, including traditional editing,
compilation, and debugging tools, as well as authoring and
other tools targeted at interactive development. He/she works
closely with product marketing, QA, Documentation and other
development groups. The Director of Tools is responsible for
overall coordination of all technical deliverables, from the
planning stage through delivery and support. Often the Director
of Tools is viewed as a second level management position that
requires hands-on technical management. Entry-Level Salary
Range: $40,000-$80,000.

New Media Director

New Media Director directs the members of the production team,
and keeps them on task. The New Media Director makes sure
that everyone has the tools, content and assets needed to do
their job. A New Media Director's place in company structure
varies. A project may go from the Producer to the Project
Director then to a team of Researchers who forward information
to Writers, who then dispatch content to the New Media
Department, where the New Media Director works with a team
of Artists, Designers and Programmers to achieve the design
objectives. Entry-Level Salary Range: $55,000-75,000.

Creative Director (Games)

The Creative Director provides the artists with creative direction
and manages their work to make certain that all artwork
conforms to design specifications and meets or exceeds the
artistic standards that have previously been established. To that
end, the Creative Director has responsibility for the overall look

and feel of games, contributing heavily to game design. The second job function involves managing the art schedule and deliverables timeline for a group of roughly 10 artists. Working closely with the Producer, the Creative Director has responsibility for ensuring that all art assets are delivered on time and that the art staff is managed efficiently. This position involves extensive, hands-on project management skills, and an understanding of, and sensitivity to, the creative processes involved in creating computer games. Entry-Level Salary Range: $50,000-$100,000.

Head of Computer Graphics

The Head of Computer Graphics is responsible for overall operation of the Computer Graphics department, including scheduling, media flow, resource management, evaluation and purchase of software and hardware. Entry-Level Salary Range: $50,000-$100,000.

Film, Stage and Television Directors

Film, Stage, and Television Directors direct the overall production, and/or specific aspects of production. They have the final responsibility for ensuring that everything is ready to be filmed or performed. Film, Stage, and Television Directors may study scripts to determine artistic interpretation, plan and arrange for set designs, costumes, sound effects and lighting, select and cast for roles in the production by viewing performances, and conduct screen tests and auditions. They instruct Camera Operators on the position and the angle of their shots, and coordinate changes in lighting and sound. They edit film or videotape, add sound tracks and other effects, and coordinate the activities of the studio/stage crew and performers.

Filmmaking is the Director's art. The Film Director usually works with one camera and an Assistant Director or two, who handle the operation of the company working on the stage or location. The Film Director studies the script, breaks it down into elements, creates the shooting schedule, and works with the Film Editor as well as the Director of Photography. Each Director works with the Production Designer or Art Director in a different way. If the project is very elaborate, with many sets and locations, the Director may want very detailed storyboards depicting each camera setup. Some Directors prefer to spend the bulk of their time working with the Actors' performances and are not so concerned with their environments, so they may not want a lot of assistance. The Director is in charge of making of the film, and must do whatever it takes to keep everyone focused on the good of the common enterprise. Entry-Level Salary Range: $50,000 – $100,000.

Spot lit still from Alias|Wavefront's *Bingo,* a 3D computer animation created by Chris Landreth

Video Director

The Video Director's job is more technically oriented than that of the Film Director. The Video Director studies the script, determines the approach, prepares a shooting schedule, does camera blocking, and rehearses Actors off and on the set. Entry-Level Salary Range: $40,000-$80,000.

Lighting Director (Live Action)

The Lighting Director is responsible for lighting a production, whether it is shot indoors or out. Often Lighting Directors double as the Cameraman on low budget productions. The Lighting Director is involved at all stages of the lighting including planning, setup, and installation of lighting. Lighting Directors may specialize in lighting three-dimensional space needed for theater subjects on a stage, or for film or video, where the lighting does not move and must be re-lit whenever the camera angle changes. Theater Lighting Directors have the opportunity to choreograph light, according to movement of the live subject on the stage. This Director works closely with the

Director of Photography. Entry-Level Salary Range: $30,000-$40,000+.

Director of Photography

The Director of Photography on a film project is responsible for the images that appear on a strip of film. This Director's creative use of cameras, film stock, lighting, lenses, filters, diffusers, camera angles, and moves gives a mood and character to the story. The end result of all the art, technology, and talent that goes into telling that story rests in the Director of Photography's hands. In preproduction, the Director of Photography helps to specify set design requirements, choose set and wardrobe colors, do site surveys, and handle equipment logistics. He or she might also assist in the details of domestic and international travel. The Director or Producer often hires the Director of Photography and works closely with them to structure a design for the project within the budget. The Director of Photography may be required to undertake the following additional tasks: organize the film production unit, instruct Camera Operators regarding camera set-ups, signal cues to start and stop filming, and view processed film after each day's filming and decide if re-filming is necessary. Entry-Level Salary Range: $30,000-$60,000.

Real World Example
Creative Director of Animation
Jay Jacobee

About the Career/Typical Duties
I basically do storyboard concepts and I oversee production creatively, to make sure that workers are on target in terms of concept, design, and schedule.

Career Ladder
Animator, Art Director, Creative Director

It's hard because I own my own company. I have worked in the animation field for about 5 years now. I have a business background as well as a creative background. You need luck and persistence. First you become an Art Director and then Creative Director. Being Creative Director is pretty much it in terms of the creative.

Education

Advertising in school helped me indirectly, but there was really more on the job training, once I got into the studios, I was trained as an Animator.

It depends on your aims. For me, I studied advertising design and it was the most lucrative choice because it taught me how to package my thoughts whether it be photography, animation, or illustration. I think when I got into animation the ad design background helped me understand storytelling and that sort of thing. It is absolutely important to go to school, having an art background, a drawing background, an advertising background—as varied a background in the arts as possible.

Salary

It ranges from $50,000 to $200,000. It just depends.

Real World Example
Director of Animation
Tim Decker

About the Career/Typical Duties

The Director of Animation is someone who oversees workers and assistants to keep the vision of the Directors and Producers alive. They oversee the animation, making sure it's within the company's standards.

Education

I got a stint as a basic cartoonist in the Air Force. I then went to Cal Arts (California Institute of the Arts). Cal Arts provided me with the education I needed.

You need a strong drawing background. If you go to an art school, I'd study drawing as much as possible. Be able to draw movement, draw quickly, and keep your shapes and volumes consistent. If you can't afford Cal Arts, then try Sheridon in Toronto, or any school that offers something in Animation. Now there are so many schools offering this. I would just go and get what you can out of it. I do believe that getting an education is important in the field. It's better because the education helps you understand the language, what's going on. You will feel more comfortable if you can move your own characters a little bit. If you experiment with animation then you will feel free to experiment with someone else's characters. A Fine Arts background is very important!!

Salary
That depends on the individual and what they are doing. Feature films pay a lot of money. I'd say they make anywhere from several thousands to at least 1.5 million. In games, we're not that fortunate.

Sources of Additional Information
Read *The Illusion of Life* by Frank Thomas and Ollie Johnson (Hyperion; ISBN: 0786860707). Also read *Film Directing Shot by Shot*, which is a good film book by Steven D. Katz (Focal Press; ISBN: 0941188108). I might also suggest *Timing for Animation*, which is good. There are a lot of jobs right now for Flash Animators, tons of them with good money. Become computer literate by learning Photoshop, Director, etc. I mean, don't be afraid of the computer. Some helpful organizations include the Motion Picture Screen Cartoonist Union, and ASIFA.

Check the following Web pages:
www.awn.com, and www.animationmeat.com

Real World Example
Video Art Director
Craig Stickler

About the Career/Typical Duties
Video Art Directors meet directly with the clients to deduce the client's needs and come up with several solutions and proposals to satisfy the client's needs. Then, upon the approval of the concepts, Video Art Directors work with Artists to communicate the ideas and help the artists bring those ideas to video, film, or print.

The Art Director is the creative liaison between the client and the Artists. I work with the client and find out what they need. Once I've done that I work with Artists to try to present the client's vision. So my job requirements are: I have managerial skills, interpersonal communication skills, a good sense of time and scheduling because there is a lot that involves just basic management, and an ability to work well under pressure.

An average day consists of 3 to 4 meetings with clients or with Producers in your company with regards to work. You have to work well in a meeting, have good communications skills. I'd say a day runs anywhere from eight o'clock in the morning to you-name-it at night, depending upon the company. The smaller the company, the longer the hours. The larger the company the more toned down hours would be. I'd say an average workweek is about 50 hours as Art Director. An average day would be coming in at 8 am, checking scheduling, finding out where everyone is as far as tasks that need to be done, finding out what meetings are scheduled for that day, talking to Artists and getting an idea of how much time they need to complete their tasks, checking email, and getting a very good idea of where things are. There are some duties that deal with basic operational tasks, like moving files back and forth. A good knowledge of network communications is important, know of working with computer files, that sort of thing. You critique Artist's work and make suggestions about what they're doing, whether they're on track or not.

Education

I suggest getting a BA or BS in Design Communication, or Graphic Design. I actually started as an Architecture student at University of Florida. I definitely recommend some graphic design education that deals with using texture and color for mood. Take painting classes and fine art classes. Look for classes with discussion in theory as opposed to practical application. The practical is necessary (hands on, using the tools, actually creating things with traditional forms of art, whether hand drawn, painted, or sculpted) but more important is theory and the concept of expression and communication through visual media. There's so much psychology that goes into Art Direction, and into invoking a mood and directing the viewer towards a certain goal. Art therapy type classes would probably apply.

I would say it is also necessary to have a good knowledge of tools. Know the tools of the Artist that you are going to be directing. Know how to do what you're asking them to do. That's the most important thing, because if you've not done it before, it's very difficult to communicate what you want done. It's much easier to explain to somebody something you have done before. One of the frustrating things as an Artist is to work with an Art Director that hasn't done what they've done, because in such cases the Art Director doesn't know how to communicate their needs. So I'd say hands on experience is crucial. Do the things that create the artwork.

Salary

$30,000-$100,000. It depends on area of the country. Entry-level art direction starts roughly around $30,000 and goes up to probably six figures.

Sources of Additional Information

Go to SIGGRAPH. I would try to get out there every single year, especially if you're going to get into video!! As far as publications, I would try the standard publications that deal with art, but I would also pick one or two relatively obscure periodicals that you wouldn't normally consider being on the bookshelves of an Art Director or a Designer.

Real World Example
Director of Traditional Animation
Bill Railey

About the Career/Typical Duties

The Director of Traditional Animation takes the initial concepts, storyboards, script, whatever, from whomever the client is, and develops it by designing characters and doing layouts. When there are bigger jobs or more jobs in house, the job can entail hiring the proper people to do necessary things, and guiding the client through the process. A Director's job is visualizing what the final picture will look like. He or she must find a way to accomplish that vision mechanically through whatever resources are available.

Traditional animation is hand drawing. The best definition is very slow motion acting; you're acting at one frame a second. You're creating believability with pencil drawing. It's 4-dimensional artwork. You have height, width, and depth, but you also have the information of time.

If we're just starting a job, we run around holding hands with a client. We need to find out what they want, how to get it done, and get resources to do it. We spend a long period of time going frame-by-frame, second by second, putting it together, doing pencil tests, doing color tests, and getting approvals. In postproduction we finish shooting on film, do color corrections, do final editing, transfer to tape, and get in sync with the clients. So we're really doing different things at different times depending on what stage of the job we're in.

Education
I've been an Artist all my life. Cartoons are fun to draw and I can't remember ever not drawing them. It just seems like a way of making money doing something that's fun. I made a short film for myself, and I took it, along with some flyers of my paintings, around to Animation Studios. I happened to hit one at the moment when they fired a Designer and I got hired as an Apprentice Layout Artist. I spent three years learning on staff.

Importance of Fine Arts background: In real life, I am a Fine Artist, so I want to say it's really important. But, realistically it's probably not that important; it does give you good perspective and you tend to have a broader vision that can come from a fine art background, but I know a lot of people that all they do is animation, that's the only role, so I wouldn't say that it's absolutely necessary.

I've had a lot of people come show me reels and portfolios, including kids with degrees in animation, and I look at their stuff and go "Great, how is this going to help you in the real world?" Other kids who have very little in the way of full education seem to get it. They just go out and teach themselves. Bottom line, a good school is access to resources. If you're really motivated you will find a way to teach yourself with or without the school. If you're not motivated, all the schools in the world are not going to be able to do anything for you. Buy books, buy videotapes, and do the drawings—that's how you learn the best.

A lot of studios will hire you as an intern or an apprentice. Do whatever you can convince them you are qualified for, and volunteer for every job that walks by.

Salary

Really hard to say. I've hired people on staff on a freelance basis, and it's usually paid per foot or per second. For a little animation an Animator with minimal experience could receive as little as $35 a foot, and based on 35mm, a foot is 2/3 of a second. A foot and a half is 1 second. For high-end television commercials, national accounts, I've heard people get as much as $250 a foot. You're talking a ten to one ratio from low to high-end, and obviously there can be exceptional cases well outside of that range.

Sources of Additional Information

Check the Animation World Networks at www.awn.com a Website. Also see www.nycartoons.com. There are a ton of good books, just for character animation that I would recommend. One good title is *Cartoon Animation* by Preston Blair (Walter Foster Pub; ISBN: 1560100842). He's a brilliant Character Animator, going back to Disney days. He did MGM work too. Also, there are several videotapes by an Animation Director named Tex Avery. Find them. Avery's one of the best cartoon Animation Directors ever.

Real World Example
Technical Director of Animation
Ed Gross

About the Career/Typical Duties

A Technical Director of Animation is a person who is responsible for solving technical problems of particular shots in a film, of any particular visual effects in a film. There are many types of Technical Directors. Tech Directors in small studios are responsible for many things, but in a large studio there can be many Technical Directors with their own specialty such as lighting, rendering, etc. A Technical Director could be responsible for making character setups for a Character Animator to animate with, so the Animator doesn't have to spend time creating, modeling, and setting up a character. That's the responsibility of a Modeler and Technical Director.

My primary duties are to oversee shots. The Animation Director is the creative force behind the show, but I have a lot of creative input as well. My main focus is to solve problems, if there's a particularly difficult shot or if we're combining mediums in a particular shot. For example, we combine a lot of live action photography or use special techniques like motion control photography with computer animation or stop motion. It's my duty to figure out how to composite those or combine those elements so that they work together. I'm not really responsible for character animation, but I would be responsible for special effects animation, say rain, fire, dirt, smoke, anything like that.

I deal with a lot of pretty much everything. I mean I do modeling, animation, lighting, rendering, texturing, special effects animation, particle systems, and file management. I'm also kind of like the system administrator of our department; I oversee the network and see if everything is working correctly. I have project responsibility like all the other Animators have. It's my responsibility to model certain scenes or animate certain scenes and help with their particular scenes, or help the animation Director with his/her job. It's kind of like an all-purpose position, and mostly I think it could be best summed up as problem solving.

The Technical Director is in charge of incorporating and pulling all the elements together in a scene. The title of Technical Director means that you are solving problems and putting everything together. You come in, sit in front of a computer for about 10-12 hrs, and then go home. I do a lot of just animating, modeling, lighting. We have meetings about once or twice a week to get together and discuss what needs to be done, and hand out responsibilities and stuff. I discuss workflow with the Animation Supervisor, who also shares ideas with me about how to improve the animations. We both talk about what would be best for a certain scene; I also spend a portion of my time monitoring some of the systems here making sure everything is working, updating our Pentium system software, installing new software. That's pretty much it... but a lot of the time, it's just sitting in front of a computer.

Education
I went to school at the University of Central Florida. Their animation program teaches high end animation tools such as Alias Wavefront, Maya, SGI equipment, now switched over to NT equipment.

Actually most Technical Directors in the country have a wide variety of educational experiences. I would say it is very important, number one, to get the artistic background done first. It is very important to get a good background in drawing, painting, and traditional hand drawn animation. That's where the foundation in animation lies, whether it be traditional animation using pencil and paper, or traditional animation using stop-motion. I think it's very important to have a good computer background and a good grasp of the principles of computer animation. There are principles and techniques that are unique to computer animation, as there are with no other medium. It's a very unique medium. It introduces concepts that are not present in any other artistic medium, including painting, drawing, and even film. Film is also a very important background as well. I took a lot of film classes while I was in school. I was part of the film program as well. Studying film is crucial. If you want to go into visual effects, know the visual effects background. Know cinematography, photography, lighting, staging, and acting. All of those are very central. They are the very cores of computer animation.

Salary

Salary depends on the area of the country. I would say anywhere from $30,000 to six figures, between $200,000 and $300,000 depending on where you are. If you are a Technical Director at ILM you are probably making around $200,000 a year, maybe less, maybe more. It depends on your position your range of responsibilities, and your experience in the industry. I mean Florida is going to pay a lot less than California or New York.

Sources of Additional Information

Go to SIGGRAPH events. Check www.highend3D.com, www.vfxpro.com (visual effects society site), www.aw.sgi.com (Alias Wavefront), www.softimage.com, www.ktx.com (3D studio Max), www.sidefx.com (Houdini, Light wave). A lot of software packages have news groups to participate in. I participate in a Maya Listserv, which is accessible through www.highend3D.com. Also try reading Ron Brinkman's *Art and Science of Visual Compositing* (Morgan Kaufmann Publishers; ISBN: 0121339602). Additionally, see the magazines *Cinefex, Cinefex, Link*, and *Computer Graphics World Magazine*. You might also consider researching the American Institute of Graphics Arts (AIGA).

Real World Example
Senior Technical Director
Dave Walvoord

About the Career/Typical Duties
The Senior Technical Director needs to be adept at visual communication. He or she needs to understand lighting and

composition, that kind of thing. Technical Directors also have to be strong programmers and mathematicians.

The Senior Technical Director works with the preproduction team to develop programs and techniques to solve specific problems. He/she works with the Art Department and other Technical Directors to build sets, props, and characters for animation. He or she also develops and implements the look of each object in the project with respect to texture, color, and camera shots. Once the final image is completed the Technical Director takes the final digital description of shots and runs the rendering process to create the images themselves for scan out onto film.

Education
I have UNIX Operating System experience and extensive 3D computer graphics experience in the areas of: modeling, lighting and shading, as well as experience on an SGI workstation using graphic packages. (Alias, Wavefront, Softimage). It's best to have an education in Computer Science, Mathematics, or Engineering, and an art background, which shows a thorough understanding of physical motion, weight, balance, texture and form. Professional experience as a commercial artist is a plus.

At Blue Sky, our real major responsibility as Technical Directors is to make sure that whatever we're working on can get out the door. Typically a Director will say, "I want to do this," and then the Producer looks at us and says, "well, how much will that cost?" We never tell the Director no, you can't do that. We always say, "Yes, we can do that. We can do it this way or this way. This way is going to cost you that much." We're responsible for making sure the graphics team is working and is able to deliver projects on time. That's kind of our biggest responsibility. Our more day-to-day tasks, if we're really involved, include rotoscoping, lighting, and compositing. We're really responsible for the look of the film. I do a 40-hour workweek.

My personal background was Computer Science. I was coming from a technical side. My undergraduate was in Computer Science. My Master's was in the visual sciences or visualization sciences. I continued to teach technical art courses to get a little more visual sense of what was going on.

Salary
You know, I don't know what the going salary is right now. When I was hired, the industry was so starving for people. I don't think they're paying what they were paying when I started.

Real World Example
Creative Director of Animation
Lisa Slater

About the Career/Typical Duties
The Creative Director of Animation helps set the course for visual design at design agencies. People send us script ideas and storyboards, and then they want us to describe to them how we visualize their project, what our creative interpretation would be.

We work with the Technical people in production to determine if we would actually produce specific projects. If the production method changes on the creative treatment, then we adjust the creative treatment to make it reflect what we think we can accomplish within the client's budget. After conferring with clients, we do a breakdown, estimating how we're going to produce the project. If the client likes our creative approach, and the budget, then they award the job to us. Once the job is awarded we have to work on maintaining the vision of the project. We make sure that it gets produced the way we see it.

Creative Directors work the most when projects are first starting off. Once production is actually going, once the design phase is done, then it kind of settles down into a more routine number of hours a day.

Education

Beyond the BA or BFA. in Animation or Computer Graphics, Creative Directors are expected to have excellent leadership and communication skills, strategic client skills, and some motion graphics and animation skills. Five to ten years experience managing creative teams in the interactive field is also desired. You need a strong art background, basically, a strong portfolio, and a strong sense of design. We're Art Directors as well as Creative Directors. You also need to know the Avid Editor. That's the most famous editing machine (works all on computer). You have to know about four or five editing programs, and at least five other major software programs that go hand-in-hand with your editing program. For starts a person could learn After Effects, Adobe Photoshop, Adobe Illustrator, and Director

Salary

Well, as an Art Director or Creative Director, it will depend very much on the size of the company. I believe the standard in the larger companies for a mid level Art Director is $80,000 to $100,000. If you are in a smaller company, it kind of depends on what they want pay. It can be $40,000 to $60,000. There's a wide range.

You can also freelance. Depending on your experience, you can get anywhere from $35 to $50 an hour. In New Jersey I worked for $35 an hour. In Manhattan I worked for $45 an hour. I don't work at $50 an hour. That's because I've only been in the field three years.

Sources of Additional Information
SIGGRAPH events and information can be very helpful. The
LFCA, the Large Format Cinema Association, can also be
informative. There are more art-related organizations for
designers. Pre-Art Festival is a really good animation festival
for viewing cutting edge animation.

Real World Example
Music Director
Tom Heddon

About the Career/Typical Duties
The Music Director supervises and directs the music staff. The
Music Director is the one who organizes the various music
talents to achieve a specific task. We produced a commercial
record for release this summer. It features the music of NFL
Films and some of narrator's voices and sound effects. We also
produce a music library for audio clips that can basically be
used in a manner similar to stock footage. So after we have
used our music for a few years and gotten the value out of it,
we then make it available for licensure through another
company. We produce CDs that are set up so that they're very
easy to go through and use in a television show or a
commercial. So we do pretty much everything you could do in
the music business. We produce film scores, produce commercial
records, produce a music library, have music licensing
capability, and do all our own music editing.

The Music Director's job may vary studio to studio. The
interesting thing about the job title, Music Director, is that
different people can do it different ways, depending on what a
person's background is. There are companies who do all the
different aspects of what my department does. There are other
companies who just do music clearances, and there are
companies that just do music production. NFL Films is sort of
an in-house film studio in the old Hollywood sense, like during

the 1930s when here in Hollywood everything was done under one roof. We model ourselves that way. So we do all of these different parts.

I run the music department at NFL Films. Our music department is pretty much a full service music department. We take care of a lot of different tasks, but we do basically anything that involves putting music into our shows. I have a staff that works for me that includes Music Editors, Music Supervisors, Music Coordinators, and Composers. I am kind of adept at all of those things. I started the department. It was myself and another guy who basically was just a Music Editor. I developed the music production company here. Now we produce our own music. We license a lot of material for our shows, so we have a person here who's an expert in music licensing, our Music Supervisor. The job of the licensor is to procure the legal rights to put different songs and compositions into our shows. The Music Editor's job is to actually cut the music against the picture. The same thing a Film Editor would do for the digital images a Music Editor does for the music. You also have sound design capability, and we do a fair amount of that for advertising in the local community and for the National Football League. NFL Films is a part of the National Football League and our job is to promote the game of pro football. We do that by producing television shows, television commercials, short films, and documentaries. As Music Director, it's my responsibility to make sure that everything gets done, to make sure that when our shows go out they're artistically superior and legally kosher.

Education
You need a strong portfolio, and an optional music degree. My background was in music production/composition. I worked for a music production company in New York City. In coming here to such a small department, the only other person in the department was the Music Editor. I was asked to supervise all

these roles, and as I got into it I was hiring people to do music clearances. I became very adept with the terminology and I started to understand the role, so that I was able to bring the clearance work in-house, and then hire someone to work for me who could do these clearances. But as far as music production, that being my strong suit, I was able to get that rolling very easily by myself.

Salary

The downside of the industry is that for every job available to someone on entry level, there are five people who want that job. Now there aren't five people who are qualified for that job, but no one knows that until they've been given the job. So what happens is entry level salaries can be quite low. To get in is a bit of a strain, and that can mean being a runner in a recording studio. For example, you can start out working for minimum wage at some of the best recording studios there are, but you'll be working sixty and seventy hour weeks without getting overtime. Once you've got in and you've got experience salary gets very high. NFL Films, because it's sort of outside the Hollywood or New York pay scales, works on a different level. We start higher and don't go as high. But a music editor on a feature film can make anything between $100,000 and $200,000 depending on the amount of time required to do the job. A composer on a feature film can make $600,000 to $1,000,000.

For a company like NFL Films where it's more of a salaried job, the pay scale is nowhere near those figures. The top end is probably one of the reasons so many people are willing to do the job. It's an artistic job that can be quite lucrative when it's associated with feature films. Even Music Supervisors and Music Directors in the freelance world stand to do very well. But like anything in that vein, it's sort of a hit and miss thing. If you become successful working on successful films, or successful television shows in Los Angeles, you can do quite well. Of course the cost of living there is very high as well. When I say $200,000 might be a salaried position in Los Angeles, you might not be living as well off on $200,000 as you would off $80,000 on the East Coast.

Sources of Additional Information
Well, there are organizations as a composer and a publisher that are responsible for collecting performance royalties. It's actually part of your income, which is involved with royalty payments, and as a musician there are unions. As in any kind of production in LA where you're involved in feature films, there are unions. It can be difficult to get into a union. But if you go to LA, chances are you'll get an opportunity. There's a lot of work in Los Angeles. I'm not saying you'll succeed, but there is work there and there are a lot of facilities there and there's a lot of production in general. So people will get opportunities. Once you have the opportunity it's up to your own hard work, skill, and talent to make the best of that opportunity. It's sort of a vague answer, but each position is so different. Everybody kind of defines the position differently. It's hard to answer with one general overriding concept.

Real World Example
Head of Computer Graphics
Boo Wong

About the Career/Typical Duties
I am responsible for the overall operation of the CG department including scheduling, media flow, resource management, and evaluation and purchase of software and hardware. In addition, I also produce broadcast and Web projects with 3D and 2D animation and effects, digital compositing, digital ink and paint, and Flash animation.

People in my field run the gamut from being Directors, producers, writers, illustrators and designers, Animators,

Technical Directors, programmers, and/or systems administrators. On an average day I bid on jobs, produce jobs, run the computer graphics department, meet outside vendors, meet students/freelancers who want jobs, and visit area universities. Since I am involved in bidding on jobs the only person who sees a project before me is the Sales Representative. Bidding involves breaking down the job costs and schedule. Should the job be awarded, I refine the schedule and hire the team to do it. After that, the job goes to the Producer on the job. If I am also producing the job then I liaison with the clients and work with the Director and Artists to complete the project.

Education

I have a strong base in art and science having studied Electrical Engineering, art, photography, and dance. Whether a fine arts background is important depends on your focus. It can be crucial if you are a modeler or if you want to do texture/ lighting. The technical background needed is computer programming/science/engineering for Technical Directors, Programmers and Systems Administrators.

Sources of Additional Information
Chat at SIGGRAPH

Real World Example
Head Illustrator/Designer
Bill Britt

About the Career/Typical Duties
I am basically in charge of drawing everything and watching out for jobs coming in and out. Sometimes I just make sure the printers work. I draw different things, like brochures, flyers, posters, and logos for coffee cups and Frisbees. We have small to medium size companies come in. We use Photoshop and Illustrator almost exclusively top of the line G4's.

Education

You need a BA in Visual Communication or Graphics Design.
I'm from California. I went to a school there for undergraduate.
I had an awesome teacher that could draw human anatomy
beautifully. I became his protégé. When I got out of college I
wanted to go into medicine because I had a minor in biology
and I like anatomy. So that's kind of what prepared me. I took
every art class I could find. A Fine Arts background is highly
important. The more varied interests you have, the easier it is to
hit the bull's eye for marketing interviews. Be well rounded.

Salary

Salary starts at $30,000 and goes up. I kept having to bounce
around states. If I stayed in one spot, say around here, I could
make about 45,000 at the medium. I have about 5 yrs.
experience. Salary sort of gets sketchy after that. Most graphics
companies are small.

Sources of Additional Information

You have to have knowledge of total competency on a
computer and you need to be able to draw on a computer. Be up
on the latest technology. *MacWorld* is good for learning about
Mac settings.

Real World Example
Director
Mike Wellins

About the Career/Typical Duties

At my company, we're very well known for character animation.
We're not a special effects house. We try to concentrate on
bringing characters to life through character performance, face
shifts, stuff like that. Industrial Light and Magic specializes in
special effects.

I work with Storyboard Artists on getting the story to work once we get the actual working board. I work with the client in creating something special. Basically, clients come to us wanting something that's funny and something that looks good, and my job is to ensure the project is funny, that it looks good and sends whatever message the client wanted to send. Whatever the driving force is behind that commercial, it's kind of my responsibility to make certain everything comes across. I also work with the Animators telling them what they're trying to convey. I work with the Producers too. We figure out whether the jokes coming across, and whether there are too many or too few. Time is at a premium. When we get down to certain spots that are really costly, high-end spots, the advertisement has to work. So we will time every single frame, just to get it perfect because that's what the clients are paying for. Working on a TV project, time is not nearly as crucial as far as the animation, but still, the timing and humor is very important.

Watching a lot of television makes it easier to pick apart certain aspects of a project. I usually work nine hours a day, five days a week.

Education
I was an Animator for eight years. I was an art major. I have no degree. I went to college for 8 years. I got a great education. It turns out in this business that your demo reel is the most important. You can have degrees a mile high but without a good demo reel you can't get in the door.

Salary
I'd say salary starts at the low end. An Animation Director probably starts in the $50,000's and a full-fledged Director is going to be higher.

Sources of Additional Information
Try getting information from ASIFA.

Real World Example
Interactive Director
Geoff Harrison

About the Career/Typical Duties
Primarily I do Art Direction, project management, and departmental management. I work directly with clients to discuss their project needs and help them formulate a design document, which usually details how we are going to achieve the client's objectives. I manage a department of artists, other project managers, and programmers, so I manage the development of my own projects and oversee the other projects that we are doing in the department.

Most projects come in as requests like, "We want to do a marketing piece to help us sell this product." Other times the client might ask something like, "We want to develop a training program for our employees..." It's really from the ground up with most people. We need to do strategic assessments, help write, storyboard, and design the projects. Creation of the design document precedes any of the actual production. The design document sets up design parameters and functionality parameters. It talks about the content that will be going into the finished project. The document has storyboards and design ideas that have been agreed upon by the client. Based on the design document we can efficiently produce the actual project.

Get your foot in the door at a multimedia company and make it known that you want to increase your responsibility level over time. The hard thing is getting in so you need to take what you can get and be very up front about your plans for advancing yourself. No smart employer hates ambition.

Education
I have a BFA. in Graphic Design and a BS in Mass Media Management. Study studio art and artistic theory. Being able to see interactive projects over the Web should allow students to

be much more prepared for the human factors of how people interact with computers.

If you're a programmer a fine arts background is not very important. But for project managers and artists, I think it's very important. I like to hire people that have learned to visualize in different ways. I've had good success with people with degrees in industrial design, painting, sculpting, and even theater. The key thing that fine arts graduates learn is how to think creatively.

Salary

Artists make between $25,000 and $75,000. Entry-level is usually production intensive. Senior positions, like Senior Designer, deal with clients more—they are often the reason some clients come to a company.

Additional Resources

Look into AIGA, IICS, *Communication Arts*, and Newmedia.com

Chapter 5
Supporting Artist

An artist is one who uses knowledge of color, line, and form, and their relationship to each other, in order to create a visual image. The combination of these elements allows the artist to create work that has appeal. Artists create visual and three-dimensional forms through painting, drawing, printmaking, carving, sculpting, photography, modeling, video, and computers. Their function is to communicate an impression or idea. Although many Artists pick a specialty, most can still perform a variety of basic art tasks.

Responsibilities

The artist's duties and responsibilities vary but revolve around their ability to paint, draw, and illustrate. Traditionally, a Fine Artist's responsibilities were defined by his or her artistic specialty. Traditional artists might have been expected to conceive and develop ideas for paintings, drawings, designs, or installations. They would choose a subject, decide how to approach it, and select a medium such as oils, watercolors, pencil, pastels, acrylic, or inks. Next traditional artists would prepare grounds such as canvas or board, and mix or apply colors to the surface using appropriate techniques, taking into account the relationships of line, color, design and form to produce work for publication. Sometimes they would run workshops and/or oversee community arts projects.

Top: *Eggs of Steel* concept drawing, Rhythm and Hues studios

Bottom: At work on storyboards at Curious Pictures

In the areas of computer graphics and animation, the traditional fine art skills are often used in the planning stages of the production, in designing a character for an animated film or a storyboard for an animation. They also create paintings for feature films under such titles as Matte Painter, Digital Matte Painter (on computers), and Supervisor. In the area of 3D computer animation, they may work with Technical Directors in the area of lighting and texture. The artist/support person may also perform the task of doing in-betweens on a cel animation film.

Education

Workers in this area might benefit from a BA, or a BFA. in Fine Arts, Painting, or Illustration. A degree in the arts is not a mandatory prerequisite for entering the field. Arts education simply helps individuals to acquire more confidence, skills, and a well-rounded art portfolio. One can certainly acquire the basic drawing and fine art skills in high school, or by attending an art academy or community college.

Entry-Level Salary Range

$15,000-$75,000. The beginning salary range depends on the skills displayed in a person's portfolio. Generally the budget for preproduction artwork is not generous. Fine Artist may get their jobs because of their portfolio, but the salary may not reflect the entry-level applicant's level of skill.

Areas

In-betweener (Cel Animation)

The In-betweener is an artist who draws the frames "in between" the keyframes of an animation. In-betweeners are employed at cel animation studios. They are known as the Assistant Animator's Assistants, and are given simple tasks, usually doing single in-betweens. Gradually they work up to doing three, then five in-betweens. There are very few Artists who have chosen to make in-betweening a profession. Most In-betweeners aspire to become Assistants, and eventually Animators. Entry-Level Salary Range: $39,300-$61,100

Storyboard Artist

The Storyboard Artist works with the story department drawing essential sketches for an interpretation of the story in graphic terms. This artist is usually a good Cartoonist, conceiving and developing ideas for cartoons and funny poses. The Storyboard Artist prepares rough and finished drawings, submits designs to the Director for approval, and writes notes and instructions for finishing and layout. The Storyboard Artist has an understanding of camera angles and perspective. He or she needs and the ability to do research on costumes, Architecture, and landscapes. Entry-Level Salary Range: $30,500- $45,000.

Storyboard from *Eggs of Steel*, Rhythm and Hues Studios

Matte Painter

A Matte Painter is an Artist who paints background scenes for live action film. Today, most matte paintings are done on the computer. The Artist paints a background, for example a cityscape. Then the line action is shot on blue screen. Later the two shots (i.e., the background shot and the blue screen shot) are composited. The line action is thus layered over the Matte Painter's painted background. Entry-Level Salary Range: $30,000- $60,000+.

Top to bottom: *Eggs of Steel* concept drawing, Rhythm and Hues; Background artist at work at Curious Pictures

Stylist

A Stylist works in the preproduction stages of an animation project to propose the look for the entire animation. This person is usually hired for their unique artistic style. Their animation drawings are colored through the use of traditional coloring mediums such as color pencils, pastels and acrylics. Their drawings are approved by the Director and used to drum up interest in the project. Entry-Level Salary Range: $35,000-$45,000, however most are contractors.

Background Artist (cel animation)

The Background Artist creates the background for cel animation. This Artist illustrates backgrounds using such media as watercolor, acrylics, oils, pastel, and/or cutout papers. Often a combination of these media is employed to create the necessary background drawings. Most background art today is created on the computer using programs such as Adobe Illustrator and Photoshop. Many Layout Artists draw with very few details, expecting their Background Artist to articulate and fine tune the background designs. The Background Artist must be ready to do so. Most Background Artists are satisfied to make their job a career. Often the Artist is not a Cartoonist but a person with extensive fine art education or illustration training. The characters, inked and painted on acetate called celluloid, are later layered over the background to complete the scene. Entry-Level Salary Range: $48,900-$169,000 (median of $89,400).

Digital Effects Artist

The Digital Effects Artist is a member of the visual effects unit. The Digital Effects Artist creates effects through the use of the computer. The effects are often referred to as "post effects" as they are done near the end of production, that is, after the animation has been created or the film has been shot. The digital effects are created and rendered separately and then composited with the live action, or computer animation sequence. Digital Effects Artists at major studios such as ILM and Digital Domain are chiefly concerned with creating a seamless blend of computer generated images and live action. Entry-Level Salary Range: $30,000-$50,000.

Texture Painter

The Texture Painter plays a crucial role in the creative process between concept and final rendered product. Texture Painters help to define the surface qualities of characters and environments. The Texture Painter works with the lighting department to determine color scheme and textural attributes for 3D models and environments. It is a Texture Painter's job to decide, for example, if the surface of one character will be smooth, shiny, and red, while another character will be fuzzy and blue. The Texture Painter may also write programs to create unique textures. Entry-Level Salary Range: $40,000-$60,000.

Production Assistant

This person acts as an assistant around the production office. The Production Manager and the Production Coordinator assign specific tasks to the Production Assistant, so the duties vary. Entry-Level Salary Range: $25,000-$30,000.

Production Artist

A Production Artist has a working understanding of layout, type and color, and is able to take instructions from a Designer to create a computer layout. He or so should be able to work proficiently in such software packages as Quark, Photoshop, and Illustrator. The Production Artist's responsibilities also include producing final files that will transfer properly to film. Production Artists provide essential support services to the Experience Network, including graphics production, 3D rendering knowledge, HMTL editing, asset management, project

Curious Studios traditional animation area

support, document tracking, and database and extranet management. A Production Artist also builds components and templates, compresses audio and video, and may storyboard, or create charts and graphs. Production Artists who become seniors at a company may also be responsible for assisting with the hiring and training of new Production Artists. Finally, Production Artists may work with the Design Department Coordinator to delegate work, including any graphic production and presentation responsibilities. Entry-Level Salary Range: $28,000-$40,000.

Inker/Painter (cel and 2D animation)

It is not necessary to be a talented artist to become an Inker. Neatness and a firm, careful hand are the main requirements. The work of the Inker was traditionally done by women who would make inking a career. The job of an Inker is to paint the black outlines around the animated characters, as can be seen in most cel character animation. The Painter would fill in the inside colors of the character. Often working with a large range of numbered colors, the process is similar to painting-by-numbers. Since the introduction of the computer to the animation process most inking and painting has been done through the use of software programs. Entry-Level Salary Range: $18,000-$40,000.

Visual Development Artist

The Visual Development Artist's job is to explore a written or musical property under consideration for adaptation into an animated film. Working with the Feature Animation Development Department, this Artist might consider visualization of plot, conflict, and setting with the intention of manipulating the dramatic or comedic mood of an animation. Entry-Level Salary Range: $25,000-$40,000.

Mechanical Artist

Using materials received from the Art Director, the Mechanical Artist prepares art according to the Art Director's specifications. With these materials, a "mechanical" is prepared. This is done by placing up pictures and captions on an illustration board. Sometimes the Mechanical Artist is asked to execute design elements as well. One who does paste ups and mechanicals must have excellent manual dexterity, drafting skills, an eye for spacing type, thorough knowledge of reproduction techniques, and an ability to work with painstaking precision. Entry-Level Salary Range: $25,000-$40,000.

Pencil Model Sheet Artist

This Artist creates a pencil model sheet, which is a group of original pencil drawings that on one sheet illustrate an animated character in a variety of poses, wearing a variety of expressions. Model sheets are lithographed and distributed to the animation team to ensure a uniform look and feel to a character throughout a production. Entry-Level Salary Range: $20,000-$30,000.

Storyboards and concept art for *A Little Curious*

Real World Example
Freelance Storyboard Artist
Sunil Mukherjee

About the Career/Typical Duties
Storyboard Artists take an idea from somebody and convert the idea into a set of images. In the advertising world the Art Director comes up with an idea about a product, and he or she goes to a Storyboard Artist to draw out the images he/she has in mind. The storyboards would be the Art Director's visual representation to the client. Often storyboards are sequential images that tell a story. The storyboard shows step-by-step how a commercial will evolve on screen. The Storyboard will help to establish the composition and lighting of each shot.

Usually, the ad guys will come up with the idea for their ad spot—I don't know how they go through that process. By the time they contact me they usually have a sequence of events that they will describe, and I'll draw out the number of storyboards that they request to visually describe the spot. The first stage will just involve preliminary sketching to get the ideas on paper. The client will review the sketches, make necessary changes, and then I'll sketch some more. Sometimes finished sketches are enough and sometimes they really want a really finished set of storyboards that are neat, tidy, and in color. They show the storyboard to their clients, and hopefully the client is happy. If they're not, more storyboards will be drawn. Once the storyboards are finalized they go to the folks who actually produce the commercial. The storyboard work is all part of preproduction. Whatever happens after storyboarding usually doesn't involve the Storyboard Artist.

Education

I spent 4 years at the Academy of Art in San Francisco. Originally, I thought I'd study graphic design, but two semesters into my course the Director of the department thought that I had more illustrative skills and suggested that I go into illustration. You don't need to have great skills to start but you do need some passion for drawing if you want to be an Illustrator or Storyboard Artist. The best way to prepare is to keep drawing and see if you like it enough that someday you might consider it as your career.

I would recommend taking as many basic figure-drawing classes as possible. I started off with nude figure drawings. When I had enough knowledge of the human body I moved up to Clothed figure drawings. I took as many drawing classes as the curriculum allowed me. You should also take some color classes. It's a plus to have some sense of color and how it works on the canvas even as you're just learning how to draw.

When I was in college I tried everything from watercolor, to gouache, to acrylics, to oil and pastel. Don't get intimidated by any medium. Give yourself a chance to understand how they all work before you jump to a conclusion. Eventually you will find out which one works best for you.

More important than fine arts training is illustrative training. It's mostly just about being able to draw really well. Also more important than fine arts training is having a broad imagination and an ability to develop interesting concepts and ideas. Some design software is especially helpful, like Adobe Photoshop and Illustrator. It also wouldn't hurt to know some 3D modeling software. If you're going to freelance you'll need to know some basic word processing software, have some basic bookkeeping skills, etc. so that you can invoice your clients and keep track of your records.

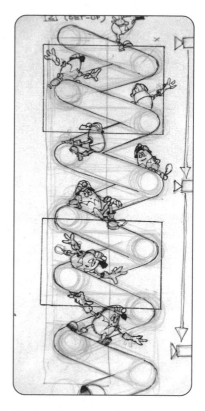

Storyboard image from *Eggs of Steel*, Rhythm and Hues

Salary

I guess that all depends on how skilled and prolific you are. Sometimes you get paid by the hour, sometimes by the number of frames. Good Storyboard Artists can draw really fast. They are also good at drawing stuff out of their heads without any reference. Advertising firms seem to be the most lucrative. They work on tight deadlines. They will come in the evening and say they want 20 storyboards by morning. In those situations a Storyboard Artist with a desperate and deadline-ridden client can really charge high fees. The price also depends on the size of your work. Quick 3x5 B&W storyboards don't command as big of a price as 4x6 color storyboards. Someone first starting out can expect to be paid $20 to $50 for each B&W 3x5 storyboard. Under tight deadlines, poster size, color storyboards can command prices at $400+ each. It comes down to deadlines, how many they want, how much time you have to do them etc. You'll need to establish your reputation as an excellent Storyboard Artist by doing the grunt work at $20 a piece before you build to charging $400 a pop!! I'm not sure how the TV and film industry pays Storyboard Artists, as I've had limited experience in working with them.

Real World Example
Visual Effects Artist/ Digital Matte Painter
George Garcia

About the Career/Typical Duties
A digital matte artist paints digital backdrops. Currently digital matte painting means painting backdrops or still illustrations on a computer. The action is composited on top of the images we create.

I do mainly digital matte painting. I also do a variety of other related tasks from illustrations of concepts, to character design, to storyboards. Say you shoot a movie in L.A. but the story takes place in Paris. You paint Parisian landscapes, drop out the background on the live action footage, and composite the actors in front of the painted landscapes so it looks like you shot the film in Paris when you actually shot it in L.A.

Education
I did my undergraduate degree in Fine Arts. It sharpens your raw talent and gets you a foundation in whatever you want to pursue in the Arts field, whether it's Web design or visual effects. A Fine Arts background is good, but if you have some specialization in mind, say in Web design, go more into that. At the very least a general study of Fine Arts is mandatory. Take courses in general art and then zero in on your specialization. Be sure you take courses in certain software, including animation or 3D software. In short, get a foundation in Fine Art and take courses in particular software that interests you.

Salary

Salary varies from place to place. It depends on what tasks you are performing.

Sources of Additional Information

Contact the Art Center in Pasadena, or studios like Disney, and they can give you direction or information. Get good magazines. Nowadays they are coming out with great magazines in Digital Effects and Computer Graphics. For example, you might check *Computer Graphics World* and *Millimeter.*

Real World Example
Graphic Artist of DVD
Mark Stucky

About the Career/Typical Duties

A Graphic Artist is someone who takes existing ideas about one particular subject to build compilations expressing whatever clients want. Every job is different. You might be creating screen for an office video, creating print, or creating titles for DVDs.

I create screens and titles for DVD's. I also do animated creative admissions between the titles. That's pretty much it. I do all the graphics work that has to be done for the production of a DVD. In most DVD productions there are 6 steps:

1 Meeting my client to arrange details of a project.

2 Producing graphics (menus).

3 Producing test disks (test).

4 Meeting with my client again so that someone can review the test disks (revisions are made).

5 Producing a master DVD to be send to the to client.

6 Client mass produces and distributes the DVD.

Education

I have a Bachelors degree in Fine Arts. I would say entry-level workers should definitely know Photoshop and Aftereffects. Knowledge of those software packages is the number one thing as far as graphics go. Illustrator is a good print program. Another program that helps is Painter. Anything else you know besides that is great, but there's your basis. I definitely recommend getting an undergraduate Degree first or at least an Associates degree. I think a Fine Arts background is good to draw upon, although it's not necessary by any means. The traditional background is important, but there are a lot of people that I know that work in graphics that don't have that traditional background. I guess they do all right on their own. It's all the direction you want to go with it. You can really come from any background as long as you know design and color relations, computers, and things like that. Definitely know video, know the different tape formats, and know the computer. You don't really have to know how to program, but know the software and programs, and know the video world.

Salary

Estimating salary is tough. It's pretty much different based on where you're at. You'll probably get more on the west coast than east. It's pretty much on an individual basis now. I found out that numbers really don't mean anything unless you're in a union, and the only unions are out in L.A. It's just all individual. It's what you can negotiate based on your portfolio and the employer's needs.

Sources of Additional Information

It's best to have a good variety of resources, both historic and modern. Read books, especially books about art history. Read magazines regarding print, graphics, new media, etc. Check *Computer Graphics World*. That's a good one. The Internet has some good resources too. Get involved with software user groups, and look at advertiser Websites. The Internet is the single most important tool a student can have in today's workplace. Know it well.

Real World Example
Digital Effects Artist
Judith Crow

About the Career/Typical Duties
Digital Effects Artists create visual effects through the use of digital effects software programs. As a member of the visual effects unit, the Digital Effects Artist creates effects through the use of the computer. The effects that the digital artist creates are referred to as "post effects" because they are done near the end of production, that is, after the animation has been created or the film has been shot. The digital effects are created and rendered as a separate file and then composited with the live action or animation sequence. Digital Effects Artists at major studios such as ILM and Digital Domain are chiefly concerned with creating seamless blends of computer-generated images and live action.

This career option requires individuals to work in team environments for the purpose of creating visual effects. The team is often referred to as a unit and may be comprised of variously skilled personnel.

Daily duties very much depend on whether or not I'm actually working on a project or not. There are sometimes periods when we're in between projects or I'm not actually responsible for one. If I'm not working on a project I print specialty jobs, help manage people, or help in general development of the technical pipeline. I spend most of my day going around seeing what the other effects artists are doing, giving them guidance, telling them what the scheduling department thinks. I mean most of the time you're looking at a screen and trying to get color right, so the viewing position is usually very, very dark. You spend a lot of time talking to other people about what's going on, sharing information. So it's casual work.

The usual day varies a lot. It can be a 10 or 11-hour day, but if it's a tense stage in the project, I'll be here Monday through Friday, maybe even Sunday. I try not to do twelve-hour days during the week because I like to spend as much time as I can with my son.

Education

Get a college degree and create a strong portfolio in traditional animation. Having some knowledge of computer animation software is ideal. Get experience in the film industry. You don't necessarily need a degree and don't have to have official qualifications. It's just something that you build up to. If you stay with one company for a long time then they know your work. They won't need to see a reel necessarily. You just get promoted by being with the company for a long time and doing good work.

Salary

New hires can expect to make $30,000 to $50,000+ to start. The starting salary depends on the quality of the portfolio, and also on company, and location. According to a Digital Effects Artist at Digital Domain, in California, "Students with a good reel could start at about, $40,000." And I'd say $40,000 very loosely. They might not get hired for that much, but a lot of people don't come in as Effects Artists. They come in as Technical Assistants, or help with computers to back things up, allocate disk space, etc. New employees work like that for a year, just to get to know how things operate. The pay is a lot less, but it's just an investment you have to be prepared to make. After a certain amount of time your pay gets better than average.

Sources of Additional Information
Go to SIGGRAPH

Real World Example
Cel Inker
Polly Bennett

About the Career/Typical Duties
Cel Inkers work on art production and design of traditional
style animation. I often work with my husband and he will
usually design the character. I will scan the design into my
computer. I digitally paint the characters for use on the Internet
and for color copies. Then I design the cel art and bookmark the
art for hand production. I hand ink each cel or bookmark and
hand paint them. I matte and frame each animation cel and
bag each bookmark. I also write children's books using my
PagePal characters.

Education
You need knowledge of the cartoon industry, animation
production, digital imaging, Web design, and management.

Salary
In the cartoon industry, after an art or animation degree, pay
usually starts low, as an unpaid intern. Later you get hired for a
paid position.

Chapter 6
Editors

Editors are often viewed as
Directors in training because
they work with the Director to
determine the final sequence
of shots for a movie. Editors
are in the postproduction
department, meaning that the
bulk of their work gets started

NonLinear editing at Curious Pictures

after the production process has been completed. Most Editors
work on non-linear computer editing systems. Others edit using
linear editing devices. Editors must operate under tight
deadlines. They must often pick up the slack of the production
department. Most editing jobs are received through outsourcing
production companies.

Responsibilities
Editors are responsible for combining various pieces of a story
into a proper sequence. They trim shots to make them fit, and
correct mistakes made during the production.

Education
A Bachelors of Arts in video production, film, or computer
graphics is helpful. Editors must learn to arrange shots to tell a
story. The must also learn to identify and cut out extraneous
material in a shot. Most of the training necessary for becoming
a video editor can be earned at a community college or at an
intensive internship. A more in-depth understanding of the
various editing styles and techniques takes time to acquire. BA
programs supply the time and space for experimentation with
style and technique.

Editor and recording system at Henninger Media Company

Entry-Level Salary Range

$20,000-$40,000 is the typical starting salary for an editor at a production studio. An Editor's beginning salary is determined by the editor's skills, and by size and location of the employing studio. Editors at major studios in metropolitan cities will earn more than their counterparts at small studios. Editors with training on high-end nonlinear editing and compositing tools can earn more, although the expense of the equipment means that these positions are primarily at larger studios, like major television stations or animation studios.

Areas

NonLinear Editor

Nonlinear editing, also called digital editing, is a lineal editing process. The NonLinear Editor uses various hardware and software tools to turn live action footage into digital data. The NonLinear Editor then edits the digitized footage. Editors of this kind often work on very expensive equipment. The NonLinear Editor edits video clips together on a nonlinear system. Entry-Level Salary Range: $20,000-$40,000.

Linear Editor

The Linear Editor edits videotape using two or more tape decks. In linear editing footage is copied directly from videotape to videotape. Unlike the nonlinear editing process, footage is never translated into digital data that is stored in a computer. The process of linear editing is known as analog editing. Entry-Level Salary Range: $20,000-$40,000.

Film Editor

Once shooting begins, the Film Editors supervise the processing of all exposed film. They prepare dailies and assemble filmed sequences. Sometimes they provide Art Directors with enlarged prints made from specific film clips (often used in promotional materials). During the postproduction period the editor does most of the work, viewing sequences and scenes with the Director, making the final cuts. The Film Editor spends most of his or her time editing and cutting film, tape, and digital content. Entry-Level Salary Range: $20,000-$60,000+.

Compositor

The Compositor is a member of the postproduction team. He or she relies on computer hardware and software to layer various individual shots together like transparencies, one on top of the next. The Compositor also deals with image processing, making necessary corrections in color and exposure to facilitate the seamless blending of various shots. Entry-Level Salary Range: $35,000-$50,000.

Technical Editor

The Technical Editor works with Technical Writers, the research and development team, and the production staff. Technical Editors help to create software manuals, in-house procedure manuals, online help systems, tutorials, and/or computer trade books. At most studios the Technical Editor is the Trainer who documents and revises the technical writing of the R&D team. Technical Editors may also work at publishing companies to edit technical trade books. Their main responsibility is to read for accuracy of information, to insure that all procedural steps are included in a given process. Technical Editors may also edit online manuals and tutorials for software companies. Entry-Level Salary Range: $35,000-$50,000.

Preparation for editing at Henninger Media Company

Real World Example
NonLinear Editor
Heather Fryling

About the Career/Typical Duties

A NonLinear Editor uses computer technology to edit video. Editing video through a computer and doesn't have to begin at the start of a film and continue progressively from there. That's why it's non-linear. You can do things in the middle of a piece and then go backwards or skip around. You can even add things to the middle without having to change everything after it.

The job changes quite a bit depending on what system you're using, and where you're editing. People come in with either commercials or something that they've shot and it's our job to get something put together for them. We usually have one-week workshops, so they come in and usually shoot Monday and Tuesday and we put everything together Wednesday, Thursday, and Friday. We don't get much time.

In the nonlinear world of editing, you're putting together all your source material into a computer's hard drive so that you can rearrange those clips, and output them into a tape. When you output the clips that's your final cut. While the clips are in the computer you can shift and move around as much as you want. In contrast, in the linear world of editing, you just conform the EDL, the list of edits that tell you what clips to use. In linear editing, clips from a source tape are recorded on a master tape. Usually you conform the EDL on the on-line suite.

After everything is shot and processed the film is transferred to beta. The beta version is brought to us so we can edit it, do sound effects, and maybe some special effects. Once we're finished working we put the final project out to beta. As far as getting it blown up or transferred to film, that's done somewhere else.

Education

I am currently going for my masters in postproduction and editing, so most of my education has been hands on or through other people giving me feedback. I have taken some workshops here, but that's about it. Usually, once you learn one nonlinear system, it's easy to jump from one to another.

Image correcting at Waveworks Digital Media

Take an AVID course. AVID is a nonlinear software system that also sells its own hardware. It's hard, because everything is changing, but if you get your hands on any kind of program and just play with it, that's the best bet. I do recommend having some type of schooling for this career. I don't think the degree has to be fully within the film or video area, or even the postproduction area, but I think workers need to have a couple classes and know the aesthetics of editing. Entry-level people should make sure they have a good technical background and good computer knowledge with PCs and MACs. Most of the advanced software programs are on MACs. I would also be real familiar with being inside a computer, like physically inside a computer.

Salary

Most of the time nonlinear and Linear Editors are freelancers. Salary can range from project to project. It can start from anything like doing something for a friend for free, to getting paid. The guys in the feature film world are probably making like $250,000+ a movie. But I am familiar with the people and salary in the Boston market, which for full time pays about $50,000 to $60,000.

Real World Example
NonLinear Editor
Kellie Cummings

About the Career/Typical Duties
NonLinear Editors organize, store, and manipulate digital information that will be used in the creation visual sequences. They do off-line compositing and sequence editing using such systems as the AVID non-linear editing system.

Let's just say that you shoot something on film. It gets transferred to video through a hardware device. Then the video gets digitized and what that means is the computer will take the video image and translate it into computer information. With your computer, everything is pixel-based. So what this digitization process does is take your video and turn it into little squares (pixels). You can only digitize from video because the video signal is electronic and can be transferred.

Once the cameraman finished his job he gives me a tape. I put the tape into the video machine and I digitize it into my computer. Once it's all in the computer my work begins. I can access the bits and clips of digital information whenever I want to. I don't have to fast-forward all the way through a tape to get at the clip I want.

Education
Get a bachelor's degree, and two years of experience in postproduction. It is important to have knowledge of all film and video postproduction techniques, including non-linear and traditional editing/recording methods. Be sure to have some experience with some of the common hardware systems.

Salary
Salary is really wide open. The thing is that an editor can make great money, but it depends who you work for. If you're experienced and you're doing commercials for McDonald's and

Nike, you are making big bucks. If you're working for those guys, you're way into six figures, but I would think that you're between $150,000 and $200,000. The money you make depends upon the types of clients you have. If you work for some really neat company, but they're only doing table slots, you won't make much at all. On salary, with benefits, low budget commercial editors might make $30,000 to $48,000 a year, and that's with experience. That's with lots of experience. Most editors start at like $20,000 or $25,000.

Real World Example
Linear Editor
Brian Cox

About the Career/Typical Duties
Well, I am given a script and I have to find the shots. We are a pretty small company, so I have a lot more aesthetic and artist license than some other editors at other production houses. I have to chose the shots and piece them together based on the scripts I'm given. I also make sure that the video and the audio in the final product all look good. I sometimes have to deal with clients, so that they can look at the finished product and tell me what they would like changed. In short, I have to deal with clients, pick out the best shots, and make decisions based on the script that's given to me.

Other than just editing the material that needs to be edited. We are pretty small company so we do a lot of overlapping responsibilities here at this company. Basically once they've shot the video and they've done the audio track, my main responsibility is to put together a program.

On an average day I come in at 9am, see what's going on, and see what deadlines are coming up. Sometimes there's not much of anything going on. Depending on what's going on, I just work till lunch and come back and work on it till 5pm. If I have a deadline I just work later at night, maybe till 9pm or 10pm. It's not a steady everyday kind of thing, sometimes there is a lot to do, and sometimes there's not much to do. On day's when there's not much to do, you can clean the decks, log the tapes and make sure they're everything is put away. So sometimes you just do maintenance things.

Education

I didn't really go to school for editing. I had to learn by doing it here, kind of as an intern. So for me it was an internship, and as far as the aesthetics of it, I watched a lot of odd stuff on television and videotape.

I would recommend going to a school that provides good facilities. Get an internship and actually do the work, because that's kind of a great way to actually learn.

A fine arts background is pretty important. Using the equipment isn't as difficult as knowing what looks good. Knowing what looked good was the part that took the most practice to get. I had to figure out what kind of composition looked best on screen, whether the timing of my shots was right, and whether I should dissolve or cut. I think that a fine arts background would be very helpful. If you have that background and you've dealt with other art forms then you've got some basis to go on when you decide what actually looks good on video.

Salary

I think anywhere from $10 or $11 an hour at entry to $100 an hour for experienced people. $100 an hour is rare. Most of the jobs pay around $20-$30 an hour.

Sources of Additional Information

There are a lot of books on film and film theory, and they really help. They talk about how to arrange images to get the effects you want, so any kind of books on film theory are usually pretty good. Read something about montage theory, like Eisenstein's books. His books talk about film form. You really just do the same thing that movie and Film Editors do, it's just that your subject matter may be different.

Real World Example
Linear Editor
Bill Holenstein

About the Career/Typical Duties
A Linear Editor is a person who edits videotape using two or more tape. The Linear Editor edits on tape from start to finish. Your source tapes are some kind of tape format, and your record deck is recording onto tape as well. Basically, you're going live through a switcher, using an EDL, and everything is going onto tape as you do the edits.

Generally we are an online production house. Online means that the show has been rough cut on a nonlinear system and has been brought into the linear realm for a final treatment because linear is higher quality. I usually get an EDL and a list of source tapes, and I conform the EDL to the way that the producer wanted the show cut based on the EDL information. That also entails coming up with credits and titles for the show. We do a lot of work for TV, especially for The Discovery Channel. We do a lot of bump ins and bump outs, basically the graphic teases that come up at the end of segments, the ones that say "Coming up next on..." We build those bumps on the online suite, and then we format the show so that it can air on television.

On an average day I come in about 9am, There's an operations department meeting, during which I find out what my jobs are for the day (ex. Today I had a show called Now Escapes, which is a show that airs on Discovery April 12, and I had to finish cutting something I started 2Days ago. I also had that on my schedule, and I had Planet Safari, which is our Planet program.

We put graphics on them to kind of fancy the show up a little bit). So I start out in the morning by finding out what I have to do. Then I get my tapes, get my EDLs, and get to work. First I take all the EDLs and run them through a program PreReader, which speeds up edit time in the online suite by facilitating the way you use the decks. Once the PreReader's done we load the tapes into the edit system. In short, you get your tapes and your decks ready, and you just start assembling the edit list if everything looks right.

When I started years ago, nonlinear editing was just getting off the ground. I wasn't as big a business as it is now. When I started there was good opportunity to get involved and get working in linear editing. I got into the game with the company that I'm with now. If you're lucky you become an assistant editor first and you spend a couple of years doing that. Depending on how well you do, you can move on to the editing position. A lot of people start out in machine rooms just loading tapes before they even get to the assistant editing position. There are a lot of jobs that people do before they even get to the assistant editing position. We have interns that come in and every now and then one of them might stay. The interns check the tapes that are going out, run errands, and that eventually leads to assistant editing. After being an assistant editor for a while you can graduate to doing graphics, nonlinear editing, or audio editing. I don't know where you could go higher than editor. Maybe you could become a producer or Executive Producer, trying to get into the production world. Other than that, you can become the senior editor of the facility, and then you're really just another editor.

Education

I don't have a communication degree or any kind of prior experience, but I have to say that there is a lot of mathematics in the linear editing field. It's just kind of logic problem type stuff. We just have to figure out things by looking at numbers. I didn't really have any specific classes geared toward editing or any kind of communication. I was actually a Political Science Major in college.

Communication classes and still photography class would be very important for learning how to frame shots and edit. Take classes with half-top platforms. I would definitely get my hands on Adobe Premiere. But really, a lot of the job is creative and it depends on how you get that creativity, whether it's just by taking classes or whatever. A still photography class would be very important and beneficial. A lot of these questions depend on where you work. Some facilities are so big that you only work on one thing your whole time there, and some facilities are so small that the workers have to do a little bit of everything. I'll go out on a shoot sometimes and do smoke or 3D graphics. It depends on where you work and what you're going to be doing, but I think a photography class is a good starting point for practicing most visual media. We do audio as well, and that's another thing.

Any kind of artistic background is handy. A lot of what you do is composition. You are compositing different scenes together, deciding how things look next to each other. It helps to have a fine arts background and a sense of mathematics.

Salary
I started working for free so the starting could be 0. I would think you never really start out. It's really hard to get into the business starting as an editor. You're not going to be able to find that opportunity at any facility that does television work. You're going to have to start as an assistant editor, so your salary starts based on how well you do at that position. I don't even want to hint at entry-level salary. The TV world is really dependent on how well your company does and what kind of

From top to bottom: Creating titles on a character generator at Henninger Media company; Editing at Henninger Media Company

business they do. People can make up to $100,000 but there are not many people that make that much. There's a lot of money in the off line, freelance field. Online editing can reach to $100,000 or more but the starting salary is not going to be close to that. You can start out as low as $20,000.

Sources of Additional Information
It is important to go to conferences. We always have someone to go out to NAB (national association of broadcasters) in Las Vegas. That's the big trade show. That's where all the companies come, like Sony, to display their latest greatest products on the market. They actually have sales reps and you can actually buy the stuff there. That's really the big trade show of this industry. There's a facility called Atlantic in Washington D.C. Once a week, they have something called Studio 650 (www.studio650.com) where speakers come and lecture. You just go and sign up and hear people talk about different issues.

Real World Example
Video Editor
Joe Baron

About the Career/Typical Duties
I do a lot of different kinds of work. I do a lot of promo work for different networks. Right now I'm cutting a half hour show for A&E. Our firm does everything, depending on the kind of editing our clients require. There's off line editing, which is where you take the footage, all the materials, screen everything, and slowly but surely put the matter into the shape of the promo with a commercial. It has to be done and that could be a one-day job through this particular job, the whole month. I mean if you work on a film, it's a 6 to 8 month session. Sometimes they'll work on one scene for a month.

The editor often works independently with the Director or producer. For the most part it's very relaxed. As you get closer to your deadlines it becomes very tense. It depends on what you're working on. If you're working on commercials there can be tension on day one. You have an assistant who usually does a lot of the housekeeping kind of duties that an editor needs done, keeping track of where everything is. Some guys know nothing about the actual computer. They just know how to use one particular program for editing. I have a little computer background and I could program, and do various things.

Most people like production. I never did because I hated standing around doing nothing, which is what production people do. I like to actually sit there and I take what everyone has done and put it into the best possible format. I enjoy it because all the vogue work is done already. I get everything and I have to make it work. The old "fix it and post" saying is only as true as your editor is skilled.

The bad thing about post is that all the money has been spent toward the production process. They're always worried about their budget, and they always try to save money at the end. At the beginning, everything is more structured. Editors often work long hours, twelve-hour days. I work a lot of hours, but for three days at a time.

Most off line is done non-linear. It used to be done non-linear. There's film editing, which I don't do, which involves taking actual film, splicing it with a razor blade, taping it together, then looking at it. And there's tape editing in which you have your videotapes, use those as sources, and record onto another tape. Then there's non-linear editing, which is disk space editing. Everything is basically dumped onto a computer disk. In old tape editing, you had to start from the beginning of the show, drop down the first shot, then the second shot and the third shot, all the way down to the end. If you made any change, you would have to reassemble everything past that

Editing and compositing at Waveworks Digital Media using Quantel Edit Box

change. In non-linear editing it's all on a disk and it's all randomly accessed. You can move things around just like on a word processor.

Education

Well, I have to be honest with you. I went to college and majored in television production, and I did not need any qualifications whatsoever." Today with increased competition for positions in this area most companies hire students with degrees in video production that have received training in nonlinear editing. At the point of graduation prospective employees won't have my years of experience, but they have the same basic skills. So it's a much more competitive business than it was, say five years ago. Kids are coming out of school knowing so much more than when I came out of school. I didn't know anything. I always hooked up with somebody who was willing to train me.

Salary

Salaries may start form $20,000. You usually start at a lower position and get trained from within. That's how most people get started. They get some kind of entry-level position either in the shipping department or the scheduling department. Then they get trained on their own time. Most places want you to learn because they know they got you real cheap and they can keep you cheap. They want you to learn as much as possible because they're not paying you well.

Real World Example
Compositor
Scott Metagr

About the Career/Typical Duties

Compositors spend most of their time merging 3D with live action, rotoscoping a lot, doing a lot of rotor work. They do a lot of work, from rotoscoping, to blue and screening. Let's say you have a 3D helicopter flying through a scene and it's going behind buildings. Compositors have to make copies of the buildings, so to speak, and put the copied elements behind the flying helicopter. I mean it depends, there's a lot of different stuff you can do. You can remove scars and make people skinnier on TV (happens a lot.) Compositing is like marrying 3D with 2D, that's all it is pretty much. Then you blend everything together. A Compositor is someone who assembles images or motion images and puts them together seamlessly. A good Compositor's work is never seen. Compositing is cool if you can imagine it. Once you understand the basics, and understand what can and can't be done, you can really come up with some fun things.

There's usually a supervisor for the set, and the supervisor will usually go over the shots during filming, making sure tracking marks are set and lighting for the green screen is correct. The film is scanned, transferred to HD or Digibeta, and brought it in on the computer. We are told what to do on the shots to prepare them. A lot of it is communication, and a lot of the responsibility is understanding the little things that make a project look right. The other responsibility is to make the scene you're working on as good as it can possibly look.

Education

I went to community college and studied filmmaking. I took one class on a Flame or an Inferno machine, and some basic Photoshop classes. I do recommend someone going to undergrad first. Take lighting classes, cinematography classes, and classes on camera work. It really helps to get an understanding of how movies are made. Understand everything that goes into a film because the goal in my mind, as a Compositor is to make the effects look like they're really there. To do that it helps to have a complete understanding of how movies work and how things should look. I recommend a

At work, Henninger Media Company

college education. Aside from gen ed, which I think is important, it's good to be in an environment where you can work with people, see what they're doing, share knowledge, collaborate, etc.

Salary

Depends on what type of Compositor you are. Flame and Inferno artists get paid a lot. Compositing is a wide range of different jobs. If you work in compositing for motion pictures and are dealing with images that are film resolution, you are obviously going to get paid a lot more than someone who is doing entry-level work. It's no reflection of skill or ability. It's just that people that work in commercials and movies will have a higher salary than people who work with community access channels or other low level projects. The salary range depends upon the software you use and the skill that you have. It could range from $35,000 to $120,000+ a year. It's cool, though, because you can travel. I just started freelancing. As a freelancer it's nice to have the flexibility, to move around and work with different people and projects.

Sources of Additional Information

SIGGRAPH, and a book called *The Art and Science of Digital Compositing* by Ron Brinkman. (Morgan Kaufmann Publishers; ISBN: 0121339602)

Real World Example
Compositor
Michael Derrossett

About the Career/Typical Duties

On an average day one of our clients shows up. Today we were working on a piece that I think will be at the Epcot Center. The project is all about the making of video games that use special capture technologies and stuff like that. Today I loaded up the footage and audio, and the client brought in some more audio. I am just synchronizing things. I'm using Smoke, which is an editing and compositing tool.

A typical day is anywhere from 7-10 hours sometimes more. A lot of it is just experimenting, placing things, rendering, checking the render, tweaking a little bit more, adjusting colors, rendering again, adjusting the lighting, tweaking more... you have to be patient. It's not a super fast process. Sometimes three weeks are spent on 15 seconds worth of video. It takes time just getting the depths of field and lighting to look right. We need to make sure there's no line around the actor or object being composited. It sounds boring to some people, but it's quite addicting.

Typically when a project gets to me it's in the final stages. It has gone through everything else. Like I said before, I work on Smoke, which is a unique tool because it's an editor and a Compositor. Sometimes I'll get audio mixes that aren't quite finished yet, and I have to finish them up. More often I get the material after it's finished, and I'm not a part of what happens before hand.

Personal Career Ladder

Compositing is a small part of my career. I view compositing as part of becoming a better filmmaker. For me filmmaking is my love and passion. I've believed that the best way to make films is to understand how everything works, to be able to talk to people and have them say "Oh wow, you're not just somebody that doesn't know what their talking about. You understand how it works." Compositing is an amazing thing. It sure is fun. It's creative and challenging. There's a nice balance of creativity and discipline. There are certain rules, technical stuff, creative stuff, that you have to be aware of. I don't know of any clear-cut path to get to a certain point in the industry. Success is just ambition and believing in yourself, and believing what you have to offer to the world, as far as creative ability, is important and good enough.

Education

Actually, I went to community college and studied filmmaking. I studied filmmaking for about six years and made some short films. I've been an avid moviegoer and a perfectionist for a long time, much to the dismay of many people. It helps to be a perfectionist when you're a Compositor. There are definitely programs that can help you, like Photoshop (for still imaging.) That software helps put things together. After Effects is another software. I work on what's called "the Smoke." I was very, very lucky because I had an internship with a company and they had a machine that nobody understood. I asked them if I could teach myself and they said "Yeah." so I could only afford not to get paid for three or four months, and I kind of taught myself how to do compositing using Flint. Because of that and my film experience I was able to get hired and work on the Smoke, which is the editing and compositing machine.

It depends where you're going to school and what's offered. Try to take lighting classes, cinematography classes, and classes about camera work. It really helps to get an understanding of how movies are made. Be able to look at a shot and say "Oh, that looks like it was shot with a 45 mm lenses." There's a lot of stuff to learn. Compositing is surely something you can do without the film knowledge, but film training helps a lot in being able to do work that blends seamlessly.

I think a fine arts background is pretty important. Like I said before, you need to have an understanding of light. Light is really, really important. Know what light is and how it interacts with things. Pay attention to shadow directions when sunlight hits something, or when shadows fall in a room. Have an understanding of how cameras work. Long lenses make people look flatter. You don't want to composite something done with a wide lens into something that was done in telephoto lens. It won't look right.

You don't have to be a total computer geek, but a fair understanding of some technical aspects is important. You have to understand how film relates to video and how video relates to film because they run at different speeds. Each medium has different characteristics so there is some math that you have to do, and you have to be aware of resolution. Whenever I have a problem of software, or when it gets into programming things, I can just call the company that makes the software.

Sources of Additional Information
The Internet is one of the best tools for research. As far as magazines go, I would say *American Cinematographer* would be helpful, and also *DV Magazine*, which is a magazine about Digital Video.

Chapter 7
Programmers/ Engineers

The Programmers and Engineers covered in this chapter are positions within the computer graphics and animation industry. They are directly involved with the creation of hardware and software. For example, they assist the artist with the technical aspects of the programs, wire systems, and programming the art for user-interactivity.

Responsibilities

Programmers write computer codes that create programs for performing specific tasks. They write the detailed instructions (programs) that tell the computer what to do to perform certain functions. Engineers help support electronic and computer infrastructures. They design and implement improvements to video, computer networks, and telephone infrastructures. They also perform maintenance procedures.

Education

Programmers need a BA or BS in computer science or information systems. The degree provides most necessary training, but is not

In training at Digital Division

absolutely required. In some cases, a 2-year AA degree is sufficient for entry-level workers. Experience through an internship or a certificate program can also strengthen the prospects for employment. Engineers require a BS in electronic engineering or computer science. Web Developers can prepare for the field by gaining experience in some or all of the following programming languages: Perl, JavaScript, Visual Basic, Visual C++, Delphi, Borland C++ builder, and Java. In most cases a four-year degree in computer science is an entry-level requirement.

Entry-Level Salary Range

$35,000-80,000. Entry-Level salary can start in the thirties if you are in a small city. Those who have successfully completed an internship can start in the forties, and are often hired by the company that issued the internship.

Areas

Technical Director of Animation (3D)

Primary duty of the Technical Director is to oversee shots. The animation Director is the creative force behind the show. His or her main focus is solving problems in cases where there's a particularly difficult shot, like when the shot calls for some combination of media (for example, the combination of animation and live action). Technical Director is responsible for modeling and animating certain scenes. He or she helps the animation Director with his job. The Technical Director is the person who is responsible for solving the technical problems of any particular shot in a film. There are many types of Technical Directors. Technical Directors in small studios are responsible for many things. In large studios there can be Technical Directors of lighting, rendering, and more. A Technical Director might be responsible for readying a character for animation, so the Animator doesn't have to spend time creating, modeling, and setting up a character. Entry-Level Salary Range: $40,000-$70,000.

Senior Technical Director

The Senior Technical Director of Animation works with preproduction team to develop programs and techniques to solve specific research and development problems. Senior Technical Directors work with the Art Department and other Technical Directors to build sets, props, and characters for animation. Technical Directors, also called "TDs," develop and implement the look of each object in project with respect to texture and color. They also design and implement the look of each shot. TDs take the final digital description of shots and run the rendering process to create the images for scanning out onto film. Entry-Level Salary Range: $60,000-$100,000.

Assistant/Associate Technical Director

The Assistant/Associate Technical Director's role is two-fold: assist the Technical Director by handling certain equipment and to act as a substitute Technical Director. Generally, the Assistant Technical Director's role is to operate special effects equipment that must be coordinated with the Technical Director's switch operation. Entry-Level Salary Range: $35,000-$60,000.

Match Move Technical Director

The MMTD's major task is to accurately animate computer characters to match the movements of live action animals. The MMTD must seamlessly blend of CGI and live action on the screen. The MMTD works with both Animators and Modeling TDs to insure accurate match moves. He or she must accurately record, use, and analyze data from production supervisors. The MMTD must perform and deliver accurate match move data on schedule. Entry-Level Salary Range: $40,000-$60,000.

Animation Setup Technical Director (Rigging Artist)

The Animation Setup TD (ASTD) designs and creates controls that define how characters can move and bend. The ASTD

Alias|Wavefront's software is used for rigging the facial expression of a character in the animation short, *The End*

provides support to these controls through each production. He or she creates specific character setups and provides support for those setups throughout the production. The ASTD identifies inefficiencies in the production process and proposes solutions. ASTDs assist in developing custom setups for a job based on studio production standards. They attend production, software, tech support, and kick-off meetings. They implement Computer Graphics Department standards. The ASTS works with departments including the software department, production department, art systems department, editorial department, and production management department. ASTDs identify studio wide needs for workshops and reference documents. Often referred to as Rigging Artists, they create virtual puppets for Animators. They build skeletons of characters. The main responsibility of this artist is to prepare the 3D computer graphics skeleton for animation. The artist must therefore solve movement problems of the skeleton and link the skeleton to the 3D computer models. The Animator then does the actual animation Entry-Level Salary Range: $40,000-$60,000.

Pipeline Setup Technical Director

The Pipeline Setup Technical Director provides direct and daily technical support to 3D and 2D productions. He or she examines problems, identifies causes, and implements solutions. The Pipeline TD creates specific job setups and provides support for the setups throughout the production. The pipeline TD identifies inefficiencies in the production pipeline and proposes and design solutions. He or she also assists digital artists with software-related problems. Pipeline TDs go on rounds with the Head TD to assist with problems. The pipeline TD implements and maintains each department's standards. He or she acts as a liaison responsible for communication issues and problem resolution. The PSTD work with various departments—including software, production, art, systems, editorial, and production management— to help identify studio-wide needs for workshops and reference documents. Entry-Level Salary Range: $40,000-$60,000.

Animatronics Engineer

The Animatronics Engineer manufactures mechanical skeletons for model characters of various scales. The Animatronics Engineer relies on hydraulics, electronics, and remote control programming to make their mechanical skeletons move. The mechanical skeletons are installed in life-size models that will now have the ability to move as the result of the mechanical implant. Stan Winston Studios used animatronics in several scenes of *Jurassic Park* to bring the T-rex dinosaur to life. Entry-Level Salary Range: $25,000-$200,000.

Visual Systems Designer

The Visual System Designer is responsible for planning technology systems in accordance with a client's wishes. They may design systems for videoconferencing, audiovisual presentations, and distance learning networks. They build strong collaborative relationships with their technical teams and clients. Visual Systems Designers document strategic decisions using text and diagrams. Entry-Level Salary Range: $45,000-$65,000.

Information Architect

The Information Architect is responsible for structuring multimedia information. Information Architects group together related bits of information so that audiences can efficiently consume the necessary content. An Information Architect constructs a blueprint for information layout. They define the program/Website goals, define their audience, identify content and functional requirements, and visually lay out their content material. Information Architects work with Graphic Designers,

Art Directors, and Creative Directors to translate the necessary content into images and text. Entry-Level Salary Range: $45,000-$65,000.

Interactive Author

The Interactive Author works with authoring software programs and writes codes that allow users to interact with computers, and/or for the computers to interact with each other. This individual may also perform hardware/software maintenance, calibration, upgrades, and installations on a wide variety of electronic media systems. Salary $35,000-$50,000.

Game Programmer

The Game Programmer is a member of a creative team that plans computer games. After the design, storyboard, and script has been approved the Game Programmer writes codes that will allow users to interact with the game through input devices like keyboards, mice, or joysticks. The Game Programmer is primarily responsible for coding and implementing such things as player controls, AI, physics, animation, and/or user interface. Game Programmers design, develop, and debug quality code. According to a strict schedule. They communicate their project needs to a Producer. They also work with the Engineers on the Technology Team. The Game Programmer must keep abreast of changes in programming languages and game style. Entry-Level Salary Range: $30,000-$45,000.

Senior Game Programmer

The Senior Game Programmer participates in game design with Producers, Designers, and Project Managers. He or she sets goals and expectations for the programming team. The Senior Game Programmer codes games based on specifications established in the design process, and re-works programming based on consumer feedback. He or she also debugs code based on QA feedback. At smaller studios the Senior Game Programmer performs both these duties and the duties of the Game Programmer. Entry-Level Salary Range: $50,000-$75,000.

Multimedia Developer

The Multimedia Developer uses design and programming skills to create interactive multimedia projects that combine sound, images, and text. These projects are interactive and are often designed for CD-ROM. The Multimedia Developer must maintain a keen understanding of the overall structure and objective of the project. The developer follows the guidelines from the Art Director or Multimedia Producer. Entry-Level Salary Range: $35,000-$50,000.

Lingo Programmer

The Lingo Programmer works with Designers and Animators to develop online gaming experiences, CD-ROMs and interactive kiosks. Macromedia Lingo is commercially available software that is a trademark of Macromedia, Inc. The Lingo Programmer is responsible for the overall development of the code, including the adjustments based on client and consumer feedback, as well as the final testing and debugging based on QA feedback. Entry-Level Salary Range: $31,000.

Flash Programmer

The Flash Programmer uses Macromedia Flash software to carry out complex designs. This Programmer writes scripts or codes to allow for user interactivity. Animation created in Flash can incorporate photo-realistic animation, vector-based animation, video, images, and documents. The flash programs can create complex and persuasive Web environments for games and/or educational tools. The Flash Programmer works in a team environment that may include technical and artistic Animators,

Sound Engineer at Waveworks Digital Media

Engineers, Multimedia Programmers, Graphics Designers, and Video Editors. Entry-Level Salary Range: $40,000-$75,000.

Multimedia Programmer

Multimedia Programmers write code for projects incorporating text, graphics, video, animation, digital/analogue photographs, audio, and 2D/3D modeling. Further specializations within this area are also possible, including specializations in video systems development, and the PC-lead programming. Multimedia programming can also be considered a sub-specialty of

Video Engineer repairs video deck at Media Vision

applications programming. Entry-Level Salary Range: $40,000-$75,000.

Audio Engineer

The Audio Engineer is in charge of a production's sound. His or she prepares the audio equipment—the audio console, microphones, tape recorders, audio turntable, and the communications systems (walkie-talkies, head sets, etc.) for production personnel. The Audio Engineer supervises the audio crew when the production is large enough to warrant an audio crew. The Audio Engineer may specialize in film, game, video, animation, or multimedia productions. Entry-Level Salary Range: $29,000-$48,500.

Video Engineer

A Video Engineer is responsible for the maintenance of television equipment. Video Engineers work closely with Camera Operators making sure that all cameras record the same colors with the same resolution. A Video Engineer works with the producer/Director to make sure all equipment necessary for a production is available and working. During a production, the Video Engineer works in the control room monitoring the quality of video signals. Engineers might also work in the repair shop. They are included on scouting trips for remote shoots during which they help pick camera placements, locate power sources, and gather information to make certain electronics will function. They are responsible for connecting equipment together, which often means running cables between cameras and remote trucks. Entry-Level Salary Range: $29,000-$48,500.

Software Developer

Software Developers provide support by designing, and maintaining proprietary tools used in animation and multimedia production. Software Developers assist Senior Software Developers as necessary. They maintain external industry contacts to keep current on recent research and industrial developments. They attend industry conferences for current information on the field. Software Developers may find employment at production studios where they may work in the Research and Development Department helping to manufacture new proprietary software. Alternatively, Software Designers might develop retail software programs for the general public. Entry-Level Salary Range: $35,000-$65,000.

Software Engineer (Programmer-Analyst)

The Software Engineer is responsible for developing, designing, writing and debugging code for corporate applications. He or she works closely with lead programmers and development teams. Software Engineers add new features to the existing product line, potentially implementing new product ideas. The Software Engineer is involved in the investigation of new technologies for integration into new software. Software Engineers apply principles of computer science to solve practical problems. Entry-Level Salary Range: $40,800- $50,000.

Web Developer

The Web Developer works with corporate initiatives to establish Websites through CGI programming. Developers are provided with input about how the site should look, feel, react, communicate, and operate. Web Developers build sites according to the specifications of their clients/employers. Although the primary focus of the developer is to program the operating systems for the site, the developer may also advise their clients about how they can best profit from the endless possibilities of the Internet. Web Developers are expected to design and color coordinate their clients' Websites, finding the best quality site host for the best price. Web Developers also assist with site registration procedures. They advise clients of promotional techniques. Entry-Level Salary Range: $38,000-$60,000.

Interface Developer

The Interface Developer troubleshoots potential digital interface problems. He or she works with technologists to bridge design and technology interests. He or she communicates technological difficulties, and tests the likely solutions. Interface Developers validate feasibility of implementing design decisions. They specify platforms, browsers, file names, and file Directory structures. They build components and templates, authoring in such languages as HTML, CSS, DHTML, XML, JavaScript, Java, PHP, ASP, ColdFusion, and Flash action scripting. In addition, Interface Developers compress audio and video, preparing for streaming media over the Internet. They create function-level interaction principles and concepts, and map intentional transaction flows. They assist in usability testing. Finally, they write create documentation and flow diagrams. Entry-Level Salary Range: $65,000-$80,000.

Internet Applications Programmer
(Internet Software Developer)

The Internet Applications Programmer adds animation and tools to a Website in order to maximize the efficiency of Internet use. Internet Applications Programmers write programs to augment Web browsers, search engines, games, chat rooms, and e-commerce sites. For example, they might create shopping carts for secure Internet purchasing from a Website. Entry-Level Salary Range: $40,000-$60,000.

Technical Service Engineer

The Technical Service Engineer sets up, configures, and maintains demonstration environments for corporate offices and tradeshows. They provide technical support for corporate and third party applications. Technical Service Engineers also plan and execute support for national and international trade shows and special events. Provide sales training and documentation for demonstration applications. Entry-Level Salary Range: $65,000.

Real World Example
Information Architect
George Olsen

About the Career/Typical Duties
Information Architects help organize the content and navigation of a Website. They are advocates for the audiences of Websites. Very simply, they help make sites easier for people to use and understand. They bridge the front-end team, which designs content, with the backend team, which designs animations.

I assign requirements developed during the strategic stage. I organize the site, organize the content and structure of the site, and develop the navigation tools that meet the needs of the intended audience. I have to figure out what's desirable from the user's standpoint. I work on the navigation, storyboarding, and

flowcharting. I figure out the best way to organize the site content, making it seem intuitive for the user. If I'm working with an existing site I might also be doing some research, doing a traffic analysis for the site. I also research emerging Web technologies in HTML, XML, etc. I consider how the new languages and programming tools might improve upon existing Websites. Part of my job is to say, "Hey, there's this really cool technology, and I think it would actually help you here." I do a lot of work creating site maps, flow charts, and other documentations.

On an average day I meet with designers, business analysts, and technology teams. We start requirements development by asking, "What are we building, who are we trying to build it for." We meet with clients. Once you have done your requirements development, you start brainstorming on ways to solve problems requiring multidisciplinary solutions. We refine those ideas into storyboards, flow charts, or documentations. We evaluate those ideas, putting together proposal based on those ideas. Then we do testing and go through another development cycle to refine the ideas. Finally we turn the project over to visual designers and back end technologies.

Education

I would recommend training in design, traditional graphic design, communication, systems analysis, and business analysis. Information Architecture is a fairly new concept so there aren't many courses on it. Fine Arts background is good. There are

Monitoring video duplications at Media Vision

people who come into the field with Journalism backgrounds, and also with IT backgrounds, but they tend to be system analysts.

Salary
I have seen salary range from $60,000 to $120,000 in major Metropolitan areas.

Sources of Additional Information
Check www.advance.iaga.org, www.nathan.com, and www.alertbox.com. Read *Designing Web Usability* and *Understanding Comics*.

Real World Example
Animatronics Engineer
Vinnie Deramus

About the Career/Typical Duties
Animatronics Engineers creating the skeletons that make characters move. For instance, if you're making an animatronic dog then you have to build a mechanical armature that will be surrounded by fur, silicon, and/or latex. It's just about being able to make a workable skeleton. Most of the engineers are very good at the things they do in this field. They can recreate an actual dog's movement with aluminum and sheet metal.

On an average day I come in and work on projects. Lets say the project is making a dog work. I come in, draft the pieces that I need to make, and then go to lab and start machining. I put the pieces together, and then its just testing and retesting whatever I made. In time you learn tricks of what to do. For example, if I need to make an eye blink, I know how to do that.

First someone makes a conceptual drawing. Then a sculpture is made. Next the project goes to our mold making department and a mold is made. Once the mechanics get a silicon skin they design the skeleton that goes inside. They work within the skin, cabling and running electronics through it. After that, it goes to fabrications and they put the fur on top. At that point the finished product is ready. It takes about 6 or 7 months.

Education

You need a mechanical background and also artistic knowledge. Take artistic and mechanical engineering in school. Learn how things move. Do personal projects on film, etc. It's pretty much self-motivation. Build a portfolio. Have an engineering background and develop your skill. Be mechanically inclined and be interested in the inner workings of the creatures. A Fine Arts background is good because you get an appreciation for what you do, a more expert understanding of where the craft originated and where its going in the future. In theater history, film history, and stage history you learn about special effects history and where it started. I wouldn't say it's required but it definitely helps. The technical background is Mechanical engineering because the engineers design and machine their own parts. If you could get into some shop classes and learn how to use machinery that would be helpful.

Salary

Salary can start from $25,000 and go upwards of $200,000 a year depending on how much of a demand there is for your work.

Sources of Additional Information

Find books on special effects. There are magazines like *Cine FX*, *Star Log*, and *Vangoria*—those are known as the trade magazines and they are very useful.

Real World Example
Interactive Author
Greg Monchak

About the Career/Typical Duties

Interactive Authors perform hardware/software maintenance, calibration, and upgrades on a wide variety of electronic media systems. They also serve as primary support for AVID system, and as liaisons between Editorial and Systems departments. They coordinate infrastructure and maintenance requirements with production schedules, and work closely with production crews to refine and improve workflow between Editorial and other production departments. Interactive Authors participate in the planning and implementation of editorial facilities. They assess technology alternatives and evaluate new equipment relevant to Editorial and Systems departments. They train users in equipment operation and procedures, and produce documentation for use in training and online reference. They also assists other video, audio, and film engineering staff as needed.

Today I was just programming all day, just straight computer programming. Some days I just do graphics. I do a lot of time-consuming jobs, like digitizing video, or rendering animations. I'll actually have a computer rendering animation for 2 Days, and I get to bill for it.

Education

Workers need to be computer and network-literate. Mac and UNIX expertise is required. Be able to troubleshoot system problems involving time code synchronization, signal path, and digital audio. You must have substantive experience maintaining and supporting professional digital media systems, including Avid Film Composers, high-end VTRs, DVD authoring systems, video projectors, calibrated audio monitors, and digital disk recorders. Be able to work well in a team environment. Also be able to prioritize and respond to multiple user requests in a dynamic production environment. Having the ability to follow through with individual assignments and initiatives is crucial. Excellent oral and written communication skills are required. Learn to be end-user and customer-oriented. Experience with shared media (e.g. MediaShare or Transoft) in an Avid environment is a plus. Experience with Quicktime authoring, DVD authoring and streaming video is also a plus. Feature film experience in an editorial support role is a big plus. You definitely need a demo CD.

Salary
The more things you have under your belt, the more money you make.

Real World Example
Rigging and Character Setup
Justin Leach

About the Career/Typical Duties
What I do is make virtual puppets for the Animators. I'll build the skeletons. I add geometric shapes to the skeleton so it looks like the figure has muscles or clothing. That's kind of what I do. It's called rigging, or character setup. I try to make an interface for the Animators to use, so the Animator can quickly get to the character and intuitively know how to use it. Sometimes I'll build special interfaces or special icons that float around the character. For example, I might make a circle just kind of lying outside the head. Someone could flex the circle and it would actually move the head around. That sort of interface saves you

from going in and trying to figure out how to move the parts you want to move. You can just click the circle, nice and easy.

Education

I did have a demo reel because I did do a thesis at Ringling but it was very minimal. I really didn't have much animation experience. My reel had some traditional animation, but I wouldn't say that I got the job because of the animation on my demo reel. I had these drawing skills, and I was perceived as a potentially good Animator, and I guess Chris Ledge felt I had a potential.

Salary

Salary used to be a lot more competitive. Generally, I've known people who started at $40,000 up to $80,000 right out of school. $80,000 is kind of an extreme case, but if you're really, really good, there are companies that are willing to pay that much money.

Chapter 8
Managers/
Producers/CEOs

This section highlights the administration side of media
production, the individuals who are ultimately responsible
for the delivery of the project in a timely manner. They oversee
the production and hire the talents necessary to accomplish
the projects.

Responsibilities

Producers, managers, and
CEOs are responsible for
funding projects, managing
budgets, and staffing the
workplace. Managers work

From top to bottom: Administrative area
at R/GA; Project Manager at Media
Vision

with their projects on a regular basis, often almost doing the
actual design and artwork necessary to accomplish a project.
The CEO, or Chief Executive Officer, is seldom ever involved in
the creative process. CEOs are more involved with practical and
administrative issues, like attracting projects and funding.
Producers are often responsible for scheduling projects and
organizing talents to ensure that production runs smoothly.

Executive Producers fund
projects personally, or locate
funding from studios or
elsewhere. The Executive
Producer also works with the
producer and Director to
assess the budget concerns of
the project.

Education

CEO's are often businesspeople, often heads of companies. A CEO of a small studio rises through the ranks and is a trained designer. He or she may not have a business degree. Producers have an understanding of the production process. Producers, managers, and CEOs require great communication skills and an ability to collaborate well in groups.

Entry-Level Salary Range

$90,000-$150,000. There is no limit to what a manager, producer or CEO can earn.

Areas

Animation Supervisor

The Animation Supervisor whether in a 3D or cel animation studio, mentors the animation team, liaisons with Producers, attends production meetings, oversees several projects at a time. He or she plans the Animator's responsibilities. In cases were the animation film is composited with live action shots the Animation Supervisor may attend the shooting to better understand the Director's vision, and to ensure that issues relating to seamless combination of animation and live action are addressed. Entry-Level Salary Range: $75,000-$150,000+.

Production Coordinator (film)

The Production Coordinator is like the second in command beneath the Production Manager; The Coordinator is one of the first people that the Production Manager hires. One of the first jobs of the Production Coordinator is to establish a home base, the actual Production Office itself. The Production Coordinator moves in any furniture, equipment, and supplies that might be necessary. They make sure everything is moved out once shooting is completed. He or she looks after the details, preparing and distributing shooting schedules, crew and cast lists, call sheets, production reports, movement orders, as well as dispensing scripts, and script revisions. Production Coordinators also make travel arrangements and book accommodations. They acquire permits and visas. If necessary, they also schedule medical examinations and immunizations for the crew and cast when filming in a foreign location. Entry-Level Salary Range: $35,000-$50,000. $45-$75/hour.

Production Manager

The Production Manager is involved in the various stages of planning, scheduling, and tracking production progress. They perform a broad range of tasks including: bidding, actualizing, and staffing. In short, they organize the logistics of day-to-day operations of the production facility. Entry-Level Salary Range: $35,000-$68,000.

Film Producer

The Film Producer generates the production and decides the style of a film. He or she is one of the most important people with whom the Production Design and Art Director work. The Producer controls the progress of a production. First, the producer has to have an idea or script to produce. Second, the producer has to have money with which to produce. Some daring producers who have no money will try to raise the money on the basis of volunteered talent and other assets. The Producer solely or collaboratively hires the production crew, including the Director and Art Director. Entry-Level Salary Range: $30,000-$100,000.

Associate Producer

Associate Producers provide administrative and professional support to a producer. The associative producer holds meetings, organizes schedules, and oversees the budget in accordance with any guidelines set up by the Executive Producer. Entry-Level Salary Range: $18,000-$50,000.

Executive Producer of Television

The Executive Producer of Television supervises multiple Producers and projects. He or she is responsible for completing projects on time and on budget. The Executive Producer is often responsible for all aspects of developing and producing television programs. His or her daily activities include but are not limited to securing funding, hiring the production heads, finding talent, and overseeing projects. Entry-Level Salary Range: $50,000-$110,000.

Film Line Producer

The Line Producer is responsible for managing *every* person and issue associated with a film. Line Producers typically work on one film at a time. They oversee the management of production from inception to completion. They supervise assistant producers, suppliers, and other staff assigned to projects. Line Producers also develop and manages budgets and schedules for projects. They manage projects to ensure that they are completed within established time frames and budgets. The Line Producer is involved in the day-to-day nuts and bolts of production finance and management. Entry-Level Salary Range: $38,000-$125,000.

Computer Aided Design (CAD) Manager

The CAD Manager manages the CAD department for an Architectural or engineering firm. He or she trains employees, coordinates schedules, and ensures that the needs of Architects and engineers have been met. This manager will also work with CAM (Computer Aided Manufacturing), which involves programming machines to assemble, paint, or otherwise process

units on an assembly line. Entry-Level Salary Range: $30,000-
$75,000.

Print Production Manager

The Print Production Manager is responsible for managing the
process of publication from concept through production and
delivery. He or she might be involved with photography, 4-color
presswork, and/or digital production. Print Production Managers
are strong project managers, juggling multiple jobs
simultaneously. Entry-Level Salary Range: $40,000-$60,000.

New Media Producer

The New Media Producer heads new media projects. He or she
locates sponsors, financiers, and the like. He or she also selects a
team to handle the tasks associated with the chosen medium.
The New Media Producer often serves as the New Media
Director as well, though it depends, once again, on the format
being used and the magnitude of the production. Entry-Level
Salary Range: $40,000-$60,000.

Multimedia Producer

Multimedia Producers are responsible for the creating and
developing multimedia projects. Multimedia Producers assign
and schedule all aspects of the project. They acquire rights to
use photos, and troubleshoot unforeseen circumstances. They
also recruit staff. The Multimedia Producer is usually familiar
with the various production tools, and is able to supervise and
inspire creativity among workers. Entry-Level Salary Range:
$35,000-$65,000.

Interactive Line Producer

The Interactive Line Producer acts as a liaison between
producers and production people. He or she monitors project
resources, staff, and financial costs. Interactive Line Producers

also coordinate the production process for Internet/Interactive products. Line Producers possess the skills and experience to excel in the following duties: organization of production requests, scheduling of projects, standardization of production processes, and communication of project needs. It is the job of the Interactive Line Producer's job to keep projects on schedule and within budget. Entry-Level Salary Range: $35,000-$65,000.

Web Content Producer

The Web Content Producer is responsible overall for the content of a Website. The content producer writes text for Websites. This often entails research into organizations missions and goals. Content Producers create text that will describe products and services that a client company offers. Web Content Producers create and edit HTML scripts. Entry-Level Salary Range: $25,000-$75,000.

Web Producer

The Web Producer takes ultimate responsibility for a Website project but does not control the design, production, engineering, or editorial aspects. It's the producer's job, through ongoing management, to help the team members communicate, work together, inspire one another, and succeed. Entry-Level Salary Range: $50,000-$75,000.

Website Manager

The Website Manager oversees the Internet projects of an organization. He or she manages database development, technical programming, Website design, and daily operations. Website Managers direct the activities of other Website staff, including Web Developers, Web authors, Web Administrators, and/or Webmasters. Entry-Level Salary Range: $30,000-$120,000.

Electronic Sound Producer

Electronic Sound Producers create music, voice, and sound effects for multimedia, computer, and/or video games. This producer integrates sound into multimedia projects, working with clips from a variety of sources including live recordings of actors, digitized sounds and effects, and synthesized music. The Electronic Sound Producer digitizes various clips and form music tracks that can be manipulated or remixed with other tracks. Entry-Level Salary Range: $35,000-$50,000.

Composer at Waveworks Digital Media

Sound Producer

The Sound Producer designs and produces the sound component of multimedia programs and products. Sound Producers work with music, voice-overs, and sound effects. They can be responsible for a variety of activities ranging from selecting or music, to digitizing, to editing recorded material. They may work with other sound professionals such as Audio Engineers, sound designers, effects specialists, digital sound processors, sound researchers, musicians, and voice artists. Entry-Level Salary Range: $25,000-$80,000.

Music Producer

The Music Producer meets with clients to select music style. Acquires approvals from clients regarding demos and revisions. The Music Producer compiles music elements for record sessions and screening sessions. He or she consults with Production and Business Affairs with regards to music contacts and budgets. He or she also reviews scripts and chooses music styles for assigned projects. Music Producers meet with Directors, producers and rights holders to discuss and define music. Entry-Level Salary Range: $30,000-$50,000.

Design Coordinator

Working with the Creative Directors, the Design Coordinator is responsible for delegating work, assisting Designers with time management, screening portfolios of potential employees, collecting timesheets, and ordering supplies. Entry-Level Salary Range: $25,000-$45,000.

PostProduction Coordinator

The PostProduction Coordinator ensures that the Postproduction process comes together in the best quality. It is vital to have someone like the PostProduction Coordinator to motivate the postproduction team towards high productivity and efficiency. The PostProduction Coordinator consults the Postproduction Supervisor on creative decisions that might arise. He or she makes certain projects are completed according to schedule. Entry-Level Salary Range: $40,000-$60,000.

Postproduction Supervisor

The Postproduction Supervisor is basically the head of postproduction. He or she takes responsibility for both the audio and video components. The Postproduction Supervisor oversees budgets and schedules, and also works closely with Producers to ensure that everything runs smoothly. Entry-Level Salary Range: $50,000-$75,000.

Real World Example
Producer of Film and Video
Ed Royce

About the Career/Typical Duties
Producers meet with clients and figure out what their needs are.
Typical needs include marketing, communications, and/or
entertainment. Producers need to be able to structure the
appropriate medium. Producers need to have a good
understanding of how the product is going to be used. They
need to know, for example, if a project is going to be on the
radio, television, or in a direct mailing. It's important to be able
to understand client's needs and pick the right medium for their
needs. Producers develop scripts. That doesn't mean you write
with but you work with scriptwriters. You go out on location
and you actually produce, whether it's for film or for video, it
doesn't matter or it's on location or in studio it doesn't matter,
you're still producing. Then you're editing the projects and you
typically, this day's in multimedia, you're involved in the
dissemination. Some of the film or video might go on the
Internet, some may go on the CD-ROM, some may go on the
video that's going to be mailed out, and some may be on
television and some on local television. So I would say
programming and distribution are important for producers to be
involved in at the same time.

An average day For me it would be meeting with clients who
have a need for video or film, it would involve scouting
locations for upcoming shoots, it would be revising, renewing
scripts, it would be editing and writing proposals and dozens of
emails in response to ongoing work.

Project stages
The stages that a project might go through before it gets to me
is the distribution and media placement, all of that stuff has
pretty much been decided before it gets to me. Most of the time

the client comes to me with a script concept and we'll then develop that concept, I'd say a lot of conceptualizing is done before it gets to me. The project's business components are already in place, meaning there's an investor and the money has already been set aside, they know when the need the project done by so that we know when they are going to use it, so those are the things that a project goes through before it gets to me. Afterwards it gets to me, as a producer you manage every aspect of the project and that included further script development, shooting, editing, timelines, deadlines, standard budgets, finding the right person, right camera man, right sound person, right graphics artist, so I'd say the key word there is "management." You manage every aspect of the project as a producer. I am the last link, I deliver the project, it's going to a TV station or an Internet developer that will put it on the Internet, or a Web Developer that will put it on a CD-ROM, and it's going to somebody that is going to distribute it or disseminate it.

Education

I have a film degree so I would say with a Communications program. I would recommend definitely courses that would help you communicate, writing is extremely important, classes that are going to teach you organization are important, and I would say some basic computer skills will be very, very important as well. I would recommend a student get an under grad first only for the purpose of communicating. Really, quite honest, I don't know if it will help if it would help with most other aspects of television production, its just that communication now is done so much via email, letters and proposal, and if you cannot communicate you will not be taken seriously, and organization is also part of communication because you can organize your thoughts and put them into whatever medium and communicate those to people. As far as learning the practical things, you will learn those on the job. The technical background needed is Basic use of computer technology, desktop computers, understand how to write documents, check emails, pull up different graphics (you don't have to be a graphics artist), but understand and know you're way around a desktop computer. If you don't you won't last a week in this program.

Salary

From entry, you'll probably going to make or be somewhere around the 30,000 yearly range and the sky is the limit after that. Really you could make a couple hundred thousand dollars a year or more than that. I'd probably say if you didn't land a sweetheart deal after just 5 years or so in the business, you would probably be at the $100,000 mark.

Sources of Additional Information

I think books, magazines, conferences, etc. aren't really going to make a dent. I think that person needs to find a mentor, find a good internship program, and take communicating or some classes in school that are going to give them some hands on so they can be familiar in being in a production environment even if its not the quality and you don't have the budget, just be in that environment, you're going to meet the right people. Find a good internship program, a good school, community college or place where you can check out equipment. Work on projects with students or other people in a collaborative study.

Real World Example
Executive Producer of Television
Tony Ceglio

About the Career/Typical Duties

The Executive Producer of Television supervises multiple producers and large projects. He or she is responsible for completing projects on time and on budget.

About the Career

It's ultimately my responsibility to make sure that shows get produced on time and to our standards. That task actually involves a set of disciplines. I write the shows. I am involved in shooting some of the segments of the shows. I direct technical. I switch and direct the taped show. I do all the hiring and stay on top of the formatting. We have production meetings once a week to talk about what we're going to do, who our guests are going to be, and what show segments we are going to include. I critique every segment, explaining what I liked and didn't like. Our objective is to inform our fans in an entertaining manner. Both my partner and I do 80 hours a week. There's a lot of P.R. work that I do. I support our marketing department pretty heavily with video. During the off- season I talk to the networks and or the local stations, seeing where our show's going.

Education

I'm a graduate of the School of Visual Arts. I have a Bachelor of Fine Arts in film. I came in as the Film Director shooting 16-millimeter film, taping practices and things for analytical purposes. In 1986 16 millimeter films went to video. Four years later I got kind of burnt out on the coaching and analytical stuff. I started writing our shows. At this point, the third season, I have fifty full-time people and about thirty freelancers. We've been very successful with our shows.

Sources of Additional Information

Check these organizations: SMPTE (Society of Motion Picture and Television Engineers), New York National Academy of Television Arts and Sciences, NAPTE (National Association for Programming Television Effects).

Real World Example
Studio Producer
Jeff Secifrodella

About the Career/Typical Duties
A Producer's job is more or less to coordinate an event, hire talent, and crew, and basically decipher the message the client is trying to send. The client's not familiar with our industry. They know what they want, but they don't know how to get there, so the producer's job is more or less to guide them. Some producers specialize in babysitting clients. A lot of the producers don't know the technical aspects of the field. I came up through the technology end and grew into the producer end. I can handle problems with the crew and equipment, plus I can handle the problems with the clients.

During a shoot you cater to the client. You're kind of interpreting what the client is telling you. If the client says that you're supposed to make something funky, it's a matter of figuring out what "funky" means. You then have to translate "funky" into film terms so that the Director and camera people know what sort of thing they should be doing.

My responsibilities include meeting with clients, and coming up with concepts for their products. I put together crews to deliver whatever the client wants. Sometimes I look for on-camera talent. It could be somebody's that's internal with the company or it could be someone that's higher, like a well-known person, a famous person to endorse the product. After you basically plan the whole production, and after it gets done, everyone else's job is also done. The cameraman's job is done, the soundman's job is done—everyone's done. The producer takes the tapes and goes into the editing room with the clients. The producer and client can work with an editor or can edit themselves. Some producers are multifaceted, but usually you go into a room with an editor. If the producer is conducting the edit, he or she knows what the client wants as the final product.

I'm based out of my home. I might meet a client at their place. I guess it would be nice to have a client come and see me, but unless you're in a production house, which most freelancers aren't, clients don't visit often. You go out to the client's building and work. You rent studios, so you really don't get a place to work. All you need is a phone and a computer.

Education

Some people I know don't know anything about the field, but yet they're good with clients. I have a background with technical equipment. Most people would go to school. I went to school for 4 years, taking communications with a concentration in film. So far, all of my jobs have been video related. Everything I learned in the video field I learned in internships, and that's about it. I learned more in my internships than I did in school as far as computer applications go.

Salary

As a freelance producer, salary ranges from job to job. I get anywhere from $250 a day to $350 a day. People can make more and people can make less. Producers can make $500 a day. Some make $1,500 a day.

Real World Example
Production Manager
Maria Boltze

About the Career/Typical Duties
The Production Manager is responsible for the processes of media production. They organize projects from planning through completion.

My primary duties are planning, scheduling, and tracking production, both within and outside the studio. I plan and track shoots, voiceover sessions, animation sequences, and video mastering. My job is to keep everyone on track, on budget, and on time. Keeping on budget requires that I be very involved in bidding and spending. I interact a lot with our clients to keep them informed about progress. I schedule approvals and reviews, and am the primary contact for general technical and quality issues. Everything that leaves the facility, including our image and the project itself, is my responsibility.

My average day stands with a production meeting so everyone understands what's being worked on, what's coming in, and what needs to get done. Then I move on to overseeing existing production. I check and review work in progress. Sometimes I help with a bid or two. Towards the end of the day I meet with clients and then clean off my desk for the next day's processes.

Education

Get a BA in Film and Video Production. I went back to school to earn a bachelors degree in film and video production. I'd always had a passion for film and moving media. Then I mustered the courage to look for a new job. I was hired at APC studios in an account management role, to locate new clients. While not the position I wanted, it helped me considerably in learning the budgeting side of production. I also learned good customer service skills. I'd strongly recommend a variety of classes in the making of film and video. Understand every aspect of what it takes to pull a production together. Know about everything from scripting, to budgeting, to lighting and camera work, to postproduction. A good Producer/Production Manager understands all the processes so they can better plan. A good internship with an organization that will allow you to watch and participate in production is always an asset. A fine arts background helps tremendously to develop your creative skill set. Creating in business situations can afford you solutions and approaches that aren't always the norm. You can, however, have a creative mind without a degree.

Salary

It really depends on whether you are salaried or not. Level of experience will also have an affect. An entry-level producer would commonly be referred to as Associate Producer and would work under someone with at least 5 years of experience. As a salaried employee I'd expect an entry level Associate Producer to earn $18,000-$25,000. An experienced producer can freelance and earn $500 or more a day, which would equate to a salary of around $100,000 if they worked every business day of the year. As a freelancer you'll work about 50% of the time. An experienced salaried Producer would therefore make anywhere from $30,000 to $50,000 depending on level of experience and employer. Various types of projects have different costs and different profit percentages. It is easier to earn a large salary in film than in audio.

Sources of Additional Information

Many industry magazines tell you a lot about what's going on in certain industries. Read *Film and Video Magazine, Mix Magazine, Interactive Magazine*, etc. Conferences aren't really all that helpful except to meet people. Organizations, like producers associations, and college clubs are great places to gain experience.

Real World Example
Line Producer
Joe Scacciaferro

About the Career/Typical Duties

A Line Producer is someone who works in the editing room. A Producer in television is expected to be a writer and developer. He or she has created a concept, and then written whatever scripts needed to be written. Then the second thing that producers are expected to do is to be a direct. Producers should to be able to go out with a camera crew or a lighting crew and get shots. Then sit down to edit and say this shot goes in here, this one goes out here.

Those positions used to be split up. There used to be Producers who were just writers. In film, television, and video, the Producer is probably the strongest creative force. In film, the Producer is really the one who puts the project together, raises the money, and hires the talents. And the Director is more of the creative force in the film.

Salary

Salary is changing. For the first five years you making under $30,000 yearly, if you can even get that. It's not a lot of money. You don't go out and get a job. You've got to jump around from job to job to make it. You keep moving. You gain as much experience as you can in as many different aspects of production as possible. Then there's a huge jump in salary. You make no money for a long time, and that just pushes out most of the workforce. The one left in the industry jump to very high positions. That's where all the money is. It's not as if every year you get 10% and somebody else is going to 15%. You develop a range of 25, 25, 25, 25, 25, $200,000.

Real World Example
Manager of Data Services
Aerie

About the Career/Typical Duties

The responsibilities of the Data Services Manager are somewhat vague because the whole high definition postproduction arena is still very much in the development stage. The biggest responsibility is getting a few projects in graphic's arena. To a certain extent, my office and my department is a big laboratory.

There's an awful lot of data testing, and an awful lot of software and hardware. Day-to-day operations typically involve scanning with the Spirit. There are really not a lot of calls for major quality graphics work in high definition code yet.

Right now it's pretty much me. I have one employee who sort of takes over some of the grub work at night, which is primarily backing things up. What's nice about high definition post is it's a very open environment. We have the ability to share information between facilities, a practice that has not always been embraced.

I try very hard to work a standard workday. That doesn't always work, but lately I've been pretty good. There have been some times when the work hours have gotten to where I'm pushing twelve hour days, but some of that has to do with my desire to make this department happen. Now I sort of feel more secure with the department. It's going to be around for a while. My hours can float a little bit, but I can get in here between 9 and 10:30, and then put in a full day. So I get out at like 5:30 or 7:00 depending on the day.

Education

Get experience, and that's really it. I have a college degree with UCLA in communication studies. It's kind of a different field. But I grew up in Los Angeles. It's sort of like growing up in Detroit and trying not to work on cars. Going to Los Angeles and trying not to work in the entertainment industry is difficult. Summer jobs lead me to production jobs in college. Production jobs tend to have twelve-hour days and go for a couple of weeks at a time. That started to interfere with school, so I then ducked into postproduction, which involves set hours. They usually run around the clock. I started out at the bottom, which would be something like logging tape, visual review tape editing, running the tape and writing down what's on it. Then from there it's taken to an editor. I went to New York to pursue some performing arts dreams. I picked up some night work as an editor, and from there I got to a point where I had a choice between continuing on the editor path, or going into film and recording, which is more craft-oriented. And there were so many people in line before me to be an editor that I chose to go into a new area that was developing. So I did that, and that gave me the experience that I needed to start this new department, which initially helped to tape and allow data on a scanner, that a big company has. And when the Spirit was able to do that, we started a new department. It's now called Data Services, which is also, sort of encompassed with high definition graphics or graphics for high definition television.

Salary

I can tell you honesty that when I started here and I was living in Manhattan I came in at $400 a week (as an editor). And I had experience. The New York market, I would say, is probably one of the more underpaid markets. The pay scale in New York is not very good. It's pretty much across the board in this industry, in my opinion. It would be the same, in my opinion, if I were to pick up and go to California, or pretty much anywhere else.

Real World Example
President of a Game Design Company
Tracy Fullerton

About the Career/Developing

Before founding Spiderdance, Inc. I worked as a producer and creative at R/GA Interactive and several other companies. I was never interviewed for a "Creative Director" position, but rather made the opportunity myself once I was at R/GA. Generally businesses are looking for "good people" in a number of fairly low or mid-level positions. I went into R/GA as a freelance interactive designer and began immediately to take on the responsibility of a Creative Director. Pretty soon, I was a

Creative Director. I find this is true for a lot of people who move up quickly—they identify a need in the company or team, begin to fill responsibilities outside of what is expected of them, and make themselves invaluable.

Current Position/Duties

My current position involves a mixture of company administration, producing, and creative direction. I also spend time looking for new clients and new projects.

My work environment is generally very casual. It has to be, as there is so much happening I need an opportunity to have some sense of relaxation during the day. I have a number of computers, PC and Mac, a dedicated Internet connection, a phone, a couch, a stereo, and a TV. For the past several years I have had the opportunity to work out of a home office. I often work long distance with Graphic Designers and programmers. I also travel quite a bit to meet people face to face.

I work way too many hours. Often I begin at 8AM and work until 10:00 or 11:00 at night. A short day would be from 9:00 AM to 6:00 PM—this doesn't happen very often.

Salary

Salary is often more dependent on experience and demand than on market standards. When I look at rate reports for the industry I know that these averages are not for top, experienced people. But such figures are a good guide for people getting out of school. When I hire people I have not worked with before I tend to pay less until I see a person's skills and experience first hand. On thing I learned that resumes and portfolios don't tell you how a person works on a team, or whether they can deliver on deadline. Resumes also won't tell you how a person works under pressure.

Sources of Additional Information

Some helpful organizations include: the Academy of Interactive Arts and Sciences, The Computer Game Developers Association, Webgrrls, and the Association of Internet Professionals.

Chapter 9
Educators/Trainers

Educators and Trainers impart knowledge about a subject area. The Educator teaches in a school environment where both theory and practice are implemented. Trainers hold practical seminars that teach people to use specific software applications or hardware. The Trainer may train in a classroom environment or on-the-job. Their program is often short term and focused.

Web training center at Digital Division

Responsibilities

The Educator is responsible for providing students with a holistic approach to learning. The Educator sets the tone of classroom interactions and must often be prepared to troubleshoot technical difficulties with equipment. Educators must plan learning objectives and set goals for their students. They are required to prepare syllabi that outline course guidelines. The Educator's job differs from the Trainer in that the Trainer solely teaches one particular software application (usually during short workshops). Trainers are responsible for learning a particular tool and teaching others how to use it.

Education

College level Educators require an MA, MFA, or PhD in Computer Graphics. Industrial Trainers have a broad education such as an undergraduate degree in Instructional Technology, Art, or Computer Science. Because they must keep up to date with the changes in software and hardware industrial Trainers often learn most of their skills through training seminars or through continuous education.

Entry-Level Salary Range
Educators-$20,000-$70,000+
Technical Trainers-$50,000-$150,000

Areas

Director of Media Services (school)

The Director of Media Services is in charge of a large inventory of equipment. The Director works with a staff of employees or volunteers, supervising these individuals, overseeing equipment use, and proposing budgets. The Director may also supervise repairs of equipment. The media service department supplies technical equipment in accordance with the needs of the faculty and students. The Director insures that faculty and student demands are met, that the students and faculty know how to use equipment properly, and that the equipment is in working condition. Entry-Level Salary Range: $25,000-$60,000+.

Animation/Multimedia Educator (Professor)

The Animation/Multimedia Educator teaches courses in animation, advises students, and serves on college committees. The professor must keep up with the changes in the field, and develop projects or research about specific areas of the field. The primary responsibility of the Animation Educator is teach courses in animation or closely related areas. The professor selects at least two courses, if full-time, that he or she would elect to teach. Every teacher has a different style of teaching, so each usually develops their own syllabus for the courses they teach. In the syllabus the teacher outlines the goals, objectives, assignments, and day-to-day activities of the course. The professor must be prepared to teach both the theory and practical application. Professors may spend ten to twenty hours per week teaching, about ten hours preparing for class, and at least two hours per week in meetings or committee related work. Their remaining time is spent researching, or developing new works of art. Professors must also hold at least two hours of office time each week during which they must be present in their office and willing to meet with students. Entry-Level Salary Range: $35,000-$75,000 for full-time Professors.

Trainer, Software Application (Trainer)

The Trainer teaches courses about specific software applications. This individual may work with a corporation, at a school, or in an adult continuing education program. Trainers at multimedia studios are used to train new employees on proprietary software programs. Trainers also teach existing employees about changes in existing software programs. Trainers may also write documentation for in house software programs. Large studios such as Pixar have established in house training centers, like Pixar University, which teach new and advanced software programs. Entry-Level Salary Range: $35,000-$55,000.

Trainer and student at Digital Division

Media Librarian (school)

The Media Librarian manages various aspects of a school library. The librarian holds seminars and teaches students and faculty to use the library systems to accomplish their research. Their educational responsibilities may include teaching students how to perform informational searches utilizing Web engines or library database software. The Media Librarian also proposes budgets for new or updated technologies. Entry-Level Salary Range: $22,000-$50,000.

Real World Example
Animation Educator
Carl Edwards
School of Visual Arts

About the Career/Typical Duties
It's an interesting mix. I try, in my classes, to create something close to a production environment. In other words, Students start a project and they have the responsibility to finish it. It is each student's responsibility to solve the problems inherent in their projects. I teach three different classes. The second year courses are primarily self-directed.

Education
I have a Bachelor's degree and about fifteen years experience. I was completely motivated to teach. It's just fifteen years of knowing precisely what to do and how to go about it.

Salary
Oh well, teaching's not a terribly lucrative area. It allows one to avoid the seasonal vagaries of production work. If one primarily does animation for toy commercials, their work is a very seasonal thing. There are times when you are busy and times when you are just dead. That's one of the nice things about teaching. It's not seasonal. A check arrives every month, so if freelance work has been slow, you can cover your rent.

Sources of Additional Information
I got terribly involved with a local SIGGRAPH Chapter. SIGGRAPH is a wonderful thing to have. It's a very important organization. Right now I'm not terribly involved with it.

Chapter 10
Writers

Writers are members of the preproduction staff for every multimedia, animation, and/or computer graphics project. They create the stories for films, and develop content for Websites.

Writers often freelance and may not be involved in the actual filming or implementation of their work. This is especially true for screenwriters. The screenwriter often sells a script to an Executive Producer, receives compensation for that script, and is then removed from the picture. The Executive Producer then hires a production team to develop the script into a movie. For writers in the multimedia area it is different. A Web Writer may be involved in the preproduction of a Web page, i.e., in developing the written content for the pages. Web Writers may also help implement and maintain a Website.

Technical Writer at Digital Division

Responsibilities
Writers' responsibilities vary from one studio to another. Their main responsibility usually involves providing documentation content for a particular media such as film, animation, or Websites. They may be involved in editing existing materials or creating documentation for new products such as software programs.

Education
Writers must read and write well. Undergraduates should get a degree in screenwriting, liberal arts, fine arts, theater, or film.

Technical Writers, such as Multimedia Writers, should understand the basics of Web design. A degree in multimedia may be most appropriate. Degrees in technical writing are also appropriate.

Entry-Level Salary Range

$35,000-$70,000 for work outside the entertainment business. Screenwriters can earn $15,000-$800,000+ on a single project.

Areas

Animation Writer

Animation Writers create the plot and gags for characters. Sometimes these writers devise new characters. Animation Writers work closely with the Director and the Storyboard Artists. Often Animation Writers confer with Directors. Some writers might write lyrics for original music written by the studio music composer. Entry-Level Salary Range: $35,000-$70,000.

Multimedia Writer

Multimedia Writers structure a project's concept into a detailed description of what happens on the screen. Writers describe what the user will see and hear while using a product. Since multimedia projects use video, and still images, sound, movement and written or spoken words to convey meaning, the writer must describe how all these components work together. The writer may also create the text that appears on the screen, or create the dialog to be spoken by actors and animated characters. The writer may generate original work for a project. The writer may also take existing work and modify it for use in a multimedia project. Entry-Level Salary Range: $30,000-$60,000.

Copywriter

A Copywriter is able to write, edit and proofread promotional material for print or electronic publications. At higher levels, Copywriters are often responsible for strategic and conceptual development of messages and stories. Entry-Level Salary Range: $36,000-$52,500.

Content Developer/Web Writer

Content Developers are responsible for the production of all textual/graphic/audio content on Websites. The Content Developer selects and proposes graphics that will enrich a Website. He or she works closely with the editor, producer, and designer of a site. Entry-Level Salary Range: $40,000-$58,000.

Technical Writer

Technical Writers prepare user documentation, reference books, and online screens that computer users consult whenever they need information about software applications. The Technical Writer may also edit manuals, illustrate and design online screens, and revise printed documentation Many Technical Writers work in-house as staff members at software companies. Others work as freelance writers editing books for trade publishers. Still others Technical Writers work for Internet based companies. Entry-Level Salary Range: $35,000-$52,000.

Chapter 11
Camera Operators

Video is a medium used to record live action or staged live action. The cameraperson operates the cameras at a shoot. Camera people often work together in the field or in the studio. On smaller field projects, one person shoots and captures both audio and video. These practitioners are responsible for capturing raw footage that can later be edited, composited, and corrected through the use of computer technology.

Camera operators work as part of a team and are often required to work long, irregular hours, including nights and weekends. They may need to travel to remote areas. For Camera Operators with considerable experience in the industry, it may be possible to become a Director of Photography. However, competition for such jobs is very high. There are few people working in this occupation.

Responsibilities
The cameraperson is responsible for building the visual content, also known as raw footage.

Education
Camera People require an undergraduate degree in video or film production. Entry-Level Salary Range: $16,000-$60,000.

Areas

Videographer (Video cameraperson)
The Videographer or Videomaker runs the camera in studios and remote locations. He or she works closely with Producers and Directors. The Videographer sometimes has a crew that includes a sound person and a lighting person. More often on smaller shoots the cameraperson will work alone gathering

footage (for example, news footage) Entry-Level Salary Range: $16,000-$50,000+.

Camera Operator (traditional animation)

The Camera Operator is in charge of shooting animation. In cel animation this means shooting action frame by frame, one frame at a time. Patience is necessary for this line of work. The Camera Operator must have sound knowledge of all aspects of animation, including knowledge of photography and lab work. The cameraperson must also know how to keep the equipment in good running order. Entry-Level Salary Range: $16,000-$40,000.

Real World Example
Videographer
Jon Fedele

About the Career/Typical Duties
Ninety-percent of the time, someone will hire you. Let's say someone important is in from out of town. So they set up the interview and then they hire you to go down and set up your lights, your audio, and your camera.

I end up working for a lot of folks. Some cable companies shoot really low budget commercials. I also work in the city for a larger cable company for which I shoot remote spots. I also do corporate stuff for companies. I work directly with corporations doing anything from taping meetings, to satellite broadcasts. Sometimes they have me come in and tape interviews.

Education
Have a demo reel and some sort of resume. I'm not sure if you really need to have a formal education. I'm sure that helps. You just really need to have a keen eye. Sometimes you're faced with different problems with equipment, like tough locations for

which it's hard to set up lighting. So you really need to be a quick thInker and a problem solver. You really need to go step-by-step if you're on location. A formal education helps because you need to know a lot of technical things. A college education definitely could fit in.

Salary

I made about $22,000 with just one client, and they needed an on staff Camera Operator so they offered me a salary. Now this is a fulltime job for me. The starting salary before taxes was 55,000.

Sources of Additional Information

Get some information form the Videographer's Association.

Chapter 12
Advice to Beginners

In this chapter professionals offer general advice to individuals entering or preparing for the field of Computer Graphics and Animation. They answer the question, "What advice would you give to a student preparing for this field?"

Digital Effects Artist at Digital Domain

Judith Crow: The most important thing that students can do is take the time to actually understand the theories about what they're doing. They need to do more than just learn particular software and hope that it will get them through. Students should understand why things work the way they do. Very often you have to sit down in front of this unfamiliar piece of software and make it work. You cannot do that unless you understand why things work the way they do. That's the best approach to solve problems.

Music Director at NFL Films

Tom Heddon: The only advice I would give to someone who is interested in music is that they should, in their educational process, make themselves a jack of all trades. You never know where you're going to get an opportunity. It's good to have as much preparation as possible. Study the technical stuff beyond anything else. Learn equipment, how equipment works, and why it works. Don't get brand specific. I can run Pro Tools on a Macintosh. Understand why Pro Tools works and how it works. You need to understand the concepts of running a workstation. Be general. Get as much technical background as you can get. When an opportunity arises don't pass it up because you feel uncomfortable. The most important thing that I can tell someone is this: be humble. It's a very difficult business and there's a lot of ego sensitivity associated with it.

Manager of Data Services at Tape House

Aerie: Learn as much computer science as you can pick up. I would say that there are a lot of professional students who don't know enough about computers. Learn computers. That would probably help you. I think there is a list of products coming out now. If you have those computer skills, you will do well. Some software packages are beginning to embrace operating systems. Computers are always getting a little bit better. You want to be in a position where you can fix your own software problems. I say learn your computer skills. It's extremely important.

Editor

Joe Baron: Most people don't go into editing, they fall into it. A lot of guys use it as a step to directing because they see how the directing process happens after shooting. They learn from mistakes of others how to better prepare for shoots. I know a lot of guys become Directors after they've edited awhile. So a lot of people use postproduction as a stepping-stone. I mean the guy who edited Citizen Caine became a big Director. He did movies, West Side Story, stuff like that. So a lot of people don't think editors make good Directors, but they usually do because they see what works and what doesn't work. I have no advice because everything is different. Just hook up with somebody who is willing to mentor you. That's what usually happens. I mean I have like three or four guys that I've worked with as apprentice assistants. Almost every editor will have a story of some guy who said, "Come here and I'll train you. I'll teach you." That's how it usually works. You always hook up with somebody.

Director/Executive Producer at Epic Vision Productions

Joe Scacciaferro- Lower your expectations. You're going to have to work. Most people don't understand that it's a tremendous amount of work. When you figure out hourly rate for what you do, you're really underpaid.

I think there are two different approaches you could take, from my point-of-view, as far as structuring a career. I know when I was in film there was a very, very small market. That was twenty something years ago. My first objective was to be able to support myself while working in the industry, as opposed to waiting tables or working as a lifeguard. I get a lot of resumes all the time and I do interview various people right out of school on a regular basis. What you need is a passion for the industry because in television itself, it's not enough to just want to get a job. It's a lifestyle, as opposed to a job. And if you enjoy it, if it's passion and you love it, it can be a very fulfilling position. If you are just looking to make money, you're probably better off somewhere else. The sacrifices and demands that this industry puts on you in terms of hours and commitment make media careers difficult to pursue it. But if you have the passion and the drive and can stick it out, you'll get where you want to be.

Inferno Artist at Stan Winston Studios

Sam Edwards: Like many other things, this industry is really competitive. There are probably a thousand people at NYU alone learning how to do this job every year. Continuing education, I know, has a program for Flame, and there are other places to go. But honestly, it is a very rare person who succeeds in finding their way into this position. I would say there are probably twenty-five new hires into a Flame or Inferno each year.

Short Film Producer

Mike Raso: If you're a student, get in touch with other filmmaking students that are older and are working on short film features. Volunteer yourself to do whatever. Carry stuff more than six hours.

Videographer

Jon Fedele: I got out of college and started working on weekends videotaping weddings. They're really tough. Try working for a cable station. The pay is definitely low, but again you get to do a lot of stuff. Watch commercials, comparing them against other things. Watch them and gain the knowledge. Then once you get some good stuff on your resume go out and start showing your demo reel. Get a high paying good job.

3D Computer Animator

Raquel Coelho: For anyone that wants to start doing animation it's nice to have as much experience as possible. Learn a lot of different techniques. Experiment with stop motion, traditional cel animation, and 3D animation. Computer animation doesn't mean that you cannot do other packages. A cel animation background is still really helpful. Go out and see a lot of films of all kinds: artistic films, commercial films, Japanese animated films, European animated films, American animated films, etc. Some people think just watching 3D is enough but there's a lot more going on. It's nice to see a lot of stuff and also to experiment with a lot of stuff.

Studio Producer

Jeff Secifrodella: If you're doing it for the money, this is not the job to be in because there are a lot of hours. It takes a long time to get to where you are making money. You spend your first year or years doing nothing but touchups. You put in the time, but don't get paid well. When you begin your career you're really low man on the totem pole. But everything you get out of this industry is what you put into it.

Senior Technical Director at Blue Sky Studios

Dave Walvoord: I found ways of contacting people who were working in the industry. I did it through alumni at my school. We'd meet at various occasions. I also got in touch with people through SIGGRAPH. I found people in the industry and I tried to talk to them and find out what they knew. I was always trying to figure out how they could help me with my projects at school/ Most of all I wanted to understand the kinds of things that they expected me to know. I felt that I was prepared. One single picture done really well can get you a job if it really stands apart. We really look for individuals who really put a lot of attention to small details in their pictures, and that's something I really see missing from most of the demo reels I watch. Effort just jumps straight out at me. There is no doubt in my mind when an individual is paying that close kind of attention to their work.

CG Animation Director at Will Vinton Studios

Mike Wellins: What we want to see is specialization in character. I would rather see some well-animated stick people having a conversation than a bunch of robots fighting. I'd say probably about 80% of the computer reels we get are robots fighting. We're looking for all phases of animation, but if you understand the basics of animation, then you can be taught all the nuances and jokes and all that.

Interactive Author

Greg Monchak: Definitely, read the books that come with the software programs. The most common mistake that people make when they get a computer program is trying and dive into it and learn from doing. Sit down and take the time to do the tutorial that comes with the program. You'll have a broader knowledge than if you had just jumped in.

Animator at Audio Vision

Dave Taylor: Be multifaceted.

Web Designer, Independent

Nick Forte: Definitely create portfolios of your work. That's so important. If you have a portfolio then you can show employers what you've done at the interview.

Computer Animator/President of Judson Rosebush Company

Judson Rosebush: Quality matters. Ideas matter. It's getting a job done. It's a lot about people. It's all about people. It's not about technology. People make things. Ultimately, it's a people business. Creativity is not as important as it is made out to be in the schools.

Rigging and Character Setup at Blue Sky Studios

Justin Leach: It takes a lot of self-discipline. The more figure drawing you do the better your skills become. Understand posing and gestures. Basically, if you have understand how humans move, that really helps. I think that is why I'm placing so much importance on figure drawing. I made contact while I was in my first year. While at Ringling, I made contact with an artist development person at Disney. I would constantly take my figure drawings and mail them off to this guy. He always wrote me back and told me what I needed to change. Then I'd do it again. It kind of tailored my portfolio to be more like a Disney portfolio. I got a lot of interviews in my last year. Learn figure drawing and make contact with someone at a company that you're interested in working at. Every company has their own requirements, specifications. They know what they're looking for.

Senior Animator at Blue Sky Studios

Doug Dooley: You know, I guess it varies from company to company. I do student advising from time to time. I have lots of advice. Research the companies you want to work for. Find out what they look for. The thing to really remember, especially with animation, is that everything revolves around your demo picks. That's what people look at. They don't even really look at the resume. I don't, anyway. Make sure that what your reel has a lot of quality, not quantity.

Clay Modeler at Blue Sky Studios

Alex Levinson: Pay close attention to art and films being made. They will greatly influence what kind of work you do. Be hungry and eager to do this kind of work. It shows. When I interview people it's the people who seem hungry to do the work that get hired. And that's the kind of thing that leads to good people. I really do believe firmly that all that we need is to learn is great art. I mean, I have history books near me and painting books and Rodin books. I keep them handy. I look at them while I work. Those are the kinds of things that I still think are very important. I really believe someone should be able to draw his or her ideas. As a matter of fact, we would like modelers to have a sculpture background. All of the modelers here do. They're all former sculptors.

Game Designer at TR Squared

Sonya Shannon: For example, right now ILM is working on that new Star Trek movie. They said to their employees, "Anybody who wants to work on Star Trek will take a cut in pay because there's so much glamour and prestige involved." Some of the big houses will pay you less because they have such a great name. There's really so much to learn. I mean, school doesn't teach you anything about meeting deadlines. You really have to put in a good three to five years in this field before you can start to call the shots yourself. That's what I found with my students, and in my own career. It just takes a lot of knocks and a lot of experience to get somewhere.

Print Advertiser at Post Perfect

Robert Bowen: Try to figure out a new angle on computer graphics. When the area gets really happening, be ready to be there. Don't go into an area like, for instance, print or Web design. Those areas are saturated. If you specialize in something unusual like robot design, then you might actually position yourself in a good spot for the future (in a diverging area.)

Character Animator at Pixar

David Tart: I definitely suggest the study of traditional animation, starting with drawing skills. It's very important. Studying acting is a very important part of animation. Learn drawing, acting, film, film structure, and story structure. It is important to be aware, aware of lighting in composition. But ultimately, it comes down to your animation skills, your knowledge of composition, acting, comedy and humor, and all those things.

Technical Director of Animation

Ed Gross: You really need to love sitting in front of the computer for twelve hours. If you don't, you will go crazy. I have really seen a lot of that. People love painting, drawing, etc. They just can't incorporate it into their lifestyle. But on the other hand, some other people just love the medium.

Another piece of advice that I would give involves self-teaching. The industry moves too fast to be taught in a school. The best people in the industry have taught themselves almost everything. It's just about picking up a manual and doing the work. Learn the software. The software is updated so fast. Every new version has maybe thirty or forty (or even 100's) of new features. You have to know that stuff and be up on all that knowledge for multiple software packages. It's just a lot of time researching and learning new tools. If you're not willing to spend the time, and if you're not excited and eager to learn those new tools, then you are in the wrong position. That's something that's really particular and unique to being a Technical Director. You need to love the technical tools. Some people really don't care about the tools that much. They don't want to master the tools. It's more important for them to animate. In that case you will be a Character Animator or a Modeler. Technical Directors are really fascinated by the tools of the whole process. I love the final product but also love learning the gadgets and computers. You have to be truly comfortable with computers. A mix of Artist and geek.

Graphic Designer at Fuszion Art + Design

Rick Heffner: Enjoy your education and take as many classes you can outside of design. Whether it's foreign language, science, or history, the creative is only part of equation. You have to know about history and life to actually apply it to your work. Just learn the foundations first. Talent, personality, respect, and trustworthiness are crucial. Employers are always looking for folks who can think outside of the box. Personality is key. In your portfolio show a variety of work, a little bit of everything. Shoe some logo work, some publication, and some illustration.

Environmental Designer at RPA

Kurt Shade: You definitely need to work on your drawing skills a lot. Your drawing skills allow you to communicate in ways that are nonverbal. The job involves a lot of working in teams. It is helpful to be able to communicate with your colleagues and potential clients in a nonverbal way. They can look at a drawing and say, "I get the idea," or "I see where you are going." Talking to someone may not communicate the ideas clearly enough for them to say, "we can take it from here." So being able to draw is extremely important. You don't need to be a brilliant illustrator, but you should be able to draw at a level that someone is able to understand. Drawing is extremely important.

Computer Aided Designer (CAD) at Onyx Group

Roderick Smith: Enjoy your education and take as many classes you can outside of design. You have to know about history and life to actually apply it to your work. Just learn the foundations first.

Web Designer at Insuractive

Michael Schreiber: Check out as many sites as you can. If you find something that you like, go into the source code to see what they've done. Designing a page is one thing, but making a page work is another. Sometimes there are tricks to it, like breaking things into tables. Have the ability to take directions. Interact with a team. In the portfolio show I would look for clean design. It doesn't take long to load. You need experience.

Head of Computer Graphics at Curious Pictures

Boo Wong: Do not be myopic. Take as many relevant classes in University as possible. For example, if you want to be an Animator, study cel, stop motion and CG animation. Take film classes so you know how lights work in the real world. Get the best internship you can and become indispensable. He necessary qualities to have are obsession, tenacity, determination, and insomnia. Make sure your portfolio has focus.

Head Illustrator/Designer at Top Hats & D'tail

Bill Britt: Drop the attitude! Be dedicated and take criticism. Have experience with logos. Create clean images with photo realistic rendering. Have competence on the computer. Kindly accept all kinds of jobs.

Director of Traditional Animation at Animagination

Bill Railey: Get a lot of experience. Find out what's being done. Focus on something: TV commercials, Web stuff, CD-ROM, feature films, etc. Pick one. Find a way to worm your way in. Make connections. Network. Good qualities are intelligence, creativity, and the ability to solve problems. Be self-motivated, self-starting, and able to say you don't know. In your demo reel, show you are able to animate well. Mimic various different styles. Show some figure drawings. Buy books, buy videotapes, and do the drawings. A lot of studios will hire you as an intern or an apprentice. Volunteer for every job that walks by.

Video Art Director at Century III Universal Studios

Craig Stickler: Absorb as much as you can with regard to your field. There's nothing more valuable than a wealth of memories based on visions that you've experienced. If you're going to be a Film Art Director then you need to watch as many films as you possibly can. There's a lot to do as an Art Director. That's outside the whole curriculum. Learning how to use paintbrush, charcoal, and digital software are aspects of it. If you don't have anything upon which to base your designs, then you've got nothing. You're just a technician. I would just subscribe to publications and magazines and read them. Just treat your brain like a sponge. Get as much input as you possibly can. Have the ability to listen. Listening is probably the most important thing. Creative people tend to be very energetic and want to express things. They're dying to express things, but they want to express things in their own way. Energy is great, but in a business setting it's imperative to meet the client need. So you have to be a good listener. You have to give the client what they want. Someone who has a very good sense of the overall package will be able to get the job done.

Linear Editor at Atlantic Video

Brian Cox: You have to be willing to work long hours from time to time. I mean it's not strictly nine am to five pm. There are days where you work twelve to thirteen hours. You're the last person that gets a project. They can take their time in writing the script and shooting, but you're the last person before the deadline. You're the one that gets crunched. You have to work long hours. An artistic background would help as much as a technical background. If the engineer's not around, you've got to be able to figure out what's wrong with equipment. The linear editing system we have runs through a computer that keeps track of the edits and the things that you've done. So you got to have some basic computer knowledge.

Linear Editor at MVI Post

Bill Holenstein: Persistence is your biggest asset. If this is what you want to do, then try to get an internship at a production house somewhere and every job they give you, do it well. Everything's a business, so if they see that you are doing well and making money, they'll be sure to elevate you to the position you want to reach. It's really important to obviously be hardworking but also to be really careful. In the postproduction, being personable with the clients is an important quality to have.

NonLinear Editor at International Film & TV Workshops

Heather Fryling: Have good computer skills, watch a lot of movies if they want to go into the feature film area. If they want to go into the documentary area then watch a lot of documentaries, see how they are cut, watch a lot of programs and movies in order to know different techniques in editing.

Some good qualities to have are good computer skills, taking criticism because a lot of people critique your films, so being able to take criticism and putting it back into your films. A demo reel should show whether or not they can edit well, using different effects, doing a lot of L-cuts, making it look really well presented, the more you do the too confusing it is, but if you're an editor, you should be able to see the different jump cuts and stuff.

Compositor at Fat Box, Inc

Michael Derrossett: Don't take it too seriously but don't take it lightly. If you want to get into, it's worth getting into, it's really exciting and rewarding, but it's the kind of thing that will make you famous, if you want respect then it is a good thing or having that "WOW" feeling. Do research, watch movies, rent DVD's if you can, or watch the making of things to find out how people have done it, research on the internet, or get a copy of After Effects. There are so many possibilities these days and it is so exciting, you can really go nuts, its so much fun.

Director of Animation at Disney Interactive

Tim Decker: Work hard and draw, keep drawing. One thing is study the figure, because if you can draw that, you can draw anything. Good qualities to have are determination, strong drawing skills, ability to work with people, team player. In reels it's nice to see walk cycles, simple walk cycles, and then run cycles. Things they've worked on in other films, I don't mind seeing that process of working, what took them to get there, you know by how they were drawing, how they were thinking, how they did the storyboards, thinking about their shots. But I really look for a strong drawing skill.

Animator at Ball n' Chain

Chuck Jepson: Practice and study movement of animals, humans, etc. Qualities to have are dedication, sense of responsibility, hard work and determination.

Graphic Artist of DVD at Grace & Wild

Mark Stucky: Learn the computer and the video, learn as much as you can, don't wait for people to come looking for you, you got to go out and find things yourself. Some qualities a graphics artist should have are good sense of DESIGN, understanding of color and motion, client skills (business sense), good grasp of video and its relation to computers, understanding of both MAC and IBM platforms, and above all you must be an expert at Photoshop/ Illustrator/ Aftereffects/ Quark/ Flash/ Director/ Painter (depending on your concentration). In a portfolio have good representations of the mentioned software and a polished presentation and steady attitude. 8-10 printed pieces, 6-8 animated pieces, all of which should have a brief oral explanation.

Visual Effects Artist/ Digital Matte Painter at CBS Animation

George Garcia: Find out if that's what you enjoy doing and check out various schools and see if you can visit various places where the work is actually done so you can see what's actually involved, so you get a better idea what it's like in the real world.

Animatronics Engineer at Henson's Creature Shop

Vinnie Deramus: It's a competitive business and pretty much a freelance type thing, it's not everyday you can get into a shop and stay there. It's pretty much a project-to-project type thing, so you pretty much need to have some more irons in the fire. The business comes and goes. The business is going up to Vancouver because it's just cheaper to shoot there than Hollywood. Good qualities to have are to be mechanically inclined, good troubleshooter and problem solver, come up with workable solutions and within time. A good demo reel should show ability that they could make something work fluently and believably, and build something efficiently using as few things as possible.

Production Manager at APC Studios

Maria Boltze: Just get out there and do stuff. Any stuff. The more variety the better. Ask questions and listen to the answers. Be assertive and take charge. A good Production Manager not only understands the many processes from audio to video, but also understands the business behind them. Pay scales, rates, budget calculations and documentation. Some good qualities to have are to have confidence and a solid knowledge base. Even if only in one field, they know they're stuff. As well, decisiveness, someone who can take charge and get the job done...no matter what it takes. Someone who's not afraid to stand up for the studio's best interest, as well as the staff and production crew. And most of all, someone who can assess and make recommendations for better process development in the future. Someone who's willing to contribute ideas. A good portfolio should have good quality work, with an attention to detail There's nothing worse than good-looking work with a typo. As well, variety as I mentioned earlier. Experience in a little of everything. Also, an honest assessment of participation on each project represented on the demo reel. Which parts they did and which they had assistance with.

Forensics Animator at Graphic Descriptions

Rudy Mantel: I would say engineering, mathematics, physics, computer and pencil drafting, and definitely 3D computer modeling and animation experience. If that's what you really have your heart set on doing, you can try to get a Forensics Animator to take you on as an apprentice or an associate to help them. That's really, to my knowledge, the only way unless, by now, some of the schools have courses in it, which I don't know of but it's possible. I would say the one quality that perhaps is the most important is accuracy. You have to be very, very accurate because any little thing that you have slipped up on, even if it has nothing to do with the fact of the animation, may be used to shoot you down and have the animation disallowed in court, because the other side of course is looking for any little thing to say "well, this isn't accurate, so what else isn't accurate?" so I would say accuracy is the most important quality. Thoroughness, accuracy, and the willingness to put in very long hours, you can't be a clock watcher because there are many times where you have to work very late into the night to get a project done.

Producer of Film and Video at Royce Multimedia
Ed Royce: Get a very good internship program and be willing to work very hard and have good common sense, don't get so caught up in a degree in academics that you forget about common sense, and look for a mentor in the business. That's probably the first bit of advice. Qualities should first be management; you need to be a good manager of time, people, and resources. Secondly, you should be creative, I don't mean you've got to be way out there on a limb as far as being creative but sometimes creativity is just ingenuity, you've got to be creative. Again I don't mean colors, and paints, and arts, but creative in working deals, creative in making things happen within a time frame, creative in knowing what sounds goods and looks good based on the objectives of the project. Organization is also at the top there. In portfolios, I look to see diversity in work, production value, so I look to see did their potential, efficiency, and effectiveness increase and rise in different types of projects and different budgets. And I really look for diversity and availability. You got to be available and

have a very diverse background. So if someone comes to me and says "I'm only available on Tuesdays and Thursdays from this hour to this hour," I say "see you later." If they come to me and say "well, I really haven't done anything" then I say " well you need to find a mentor and go get yourself in an internship program."

Clay Animator at Will Vinton Studios

JR Williams: I would say that the person who really wants to be an Animator should be aware of the difficulty of it. Learning to do it well, it's pretty obvious that animation has become increasingly popular through the years. It used to be really simple animation in films and on television was accepted by a lot of people, but with increasing usage in more and more big movies, people expect the animation to be really, really good and in order to be an Animator who can produce that kind of work, it's going to take a considerable amount of dedication and patience from that person, and also a certain amount of concentration and intensity while working to deal with that, so I think the person that really wants to do it well is going to have to experience that a little bit before they decide if they really like it or are cut out for it. Some good qualities to have are patience is definitely a virtue in this business and like I said a background or at least some kind of sense in acting ability can be important. In a good demo reel there should be high quality of animation, that is animation that is done smoothly and that was realistic in the sense of movement, as well, a general sense of sculpting ability or design ability and the ability to tell a story, the ability to just bring life into the characters.

Director of Photography at Pixar

Sharon Calahan: It is important to be able to work well within teams. It is also vital that the person be able to accept creative direction well.

Compositor, Independent

Scott Metagr: Probably get as much experience as you can on video. It's a little hard to get into the entertainment side of compositing doing film work unless you have a really good demo reel. Your demo reel is what's going to get you the job, school and stuff does help when they look at your resume but it's all about your demo reel. You got to really show something that's never been done. Some good qualities to have are the ability to work fast, get along with other people especially under stress.

Freelance Character Designer

Greg Dyer: You need to know the technical things if that's where you're going with it and get your basic drawing down very well. They want to get the concept up front and build your drawing skills very well. Look at what's out there and get a lot of references, from different areas. You might get some ideas from comics, or animations that you've already seen. It's good to have a good reference file of things. You have to be willing to change and deal with people not seeing the idea as you see it, and not get emotional about it or anything, just deal with the fact that somebody might have different ideas of how they want it so you have to give with that and a lot of it has to do with being self motivated, if you're a freelance guy. It's kind of good to have some kind of acting skills or acting background so you can get into the character and get a sense of how they move and what they would do, acting kind of helps. In a portfolio, it is good to show variety, to show a range is a good thing. Its good to get an idea of what the original concept was and get some kind of description of what the character was supposed to be.

President of Spiderdance, Inc. – A Game Design Company

Tracy Fullerton: This is a new industry and the lines between disciplines are not clearly defined in all cases. Because of this, and because of the fact that this is a highly "team oriented" industry, there are a lot of opportunities to learn new disciplines and to participate in the creative process, even when you are just starting out. My main advice would be to take every opportunity you see to learn on the job. This will make you invaluable to a multidisciplinary team. My only other advice would be to take every opportunity to learn how to work on creative teams-schools, especially art schools, tend to emphasize individual effort; companies and projects depend on team achievement.

Cel Inker at Page Pals

Polly Bennet: Complete your education. Also, attend classes in animation and other art mediums sponsored by The Motion Picture Screen Cartoonists. Get to know cartoonists if you can. You can develop some rapport with professional cartoonists by visiting their Websites. Do your unpaid internships, if possible, (that's how you get to know people in the industry who can vouch for you.) Get the best portfolio together that you can. And be prepared for rejection, you get it a lot in this industry.

Freelance Storyboard Artist

Sunil Mukherjee: Start drawing, keep drawing, and then draw some more. Also-brush up on your social and schmoozing skills-you'll need to use your charm to get clients. Some good qualities and skills to have are of course, excellent drawing skills, be able work quickly and keep deadlines, be able to listen to clients and deliver what they're looking for-(or more importantly, be able to "interpret" random mumblings about an idea into a concise series of images)-be able to "sell yourself" with schmoozing skills. In a portfolio you should be able to show that you can draw really well-and tell a story through a sequence of images. It's good to have a variety of work that shows you can work in different media and different styles. Finally, there should be plenty of "concept drawings" that show that you are creative and can come up with interesting ideas, etc.

Architect at JMGR

Jayraj Raval: It is a very, very demanding field. You have to love what you do otherwise you will never get anywhere. A lot of people here work overtime, and the reason is not only do we have to, but some people dedicate so much that you almost have to, I mean there is no way out. So if you just planning to have a 40-hour work week then Architecture is not the best field to get into. You have to be really patient because you work with the managers who are very time demanding and moody kind of people working with budgets, especially in our office there are a lot of people that you have to keep patient. You also have to be very team oriented, you have to get along with people, and you have to be very flexible. If someone is demanding a change you have to help them out. I'd look for certain things like quality not quantity, not any quantity at all but the quality of work that comes out. Nowadays everything is so budget driven; everyone wants you to do a whole lot work for less money. Detail is important, how someone details the work, because whatever you detail gets built.

Information Architect, Independent

George Olsen: Grasp of multiple fields, good understanding of writing, journalism is good training, good understanding of visual design, good understanding of functionality of what programming can do. It is a field that bridges a lot of different fields.

Chapter 13
The Portfolio Matters

In this chapter the experts provide answers to the question: "What do you look for in a portfolio or demo reel?"

Architect, JMGR Architecture Engineering
Jayraj Raval: I'd look for certain things like quality not quantity, not any quantity at all but the quality of work that comes out. Nowadays everything is so budget driven, everyone wants you to do a whole lot work and being less money. Detail is important, how someone details the work, because whatever you detail gets built.

Information Architect
George Olsen: Flow charts, story boards, written analysis, if you have a design background then show a portfolio of that.

Interactive Director at Modern Digital
Geoff Harrison: Artistic ability. I don't care what exact program's you know as much as design sense and technical accuracy.

Freelance Storyboard Artist
Sunil Mukherjee: Mostly, be able to show that you can draw really well—and tell a story through a sequence of images. It's good to have a variety of work that shows you can work in different media and different styles. Finally, there should be plenty of "concept drawings" that show that you are creative and can come up with interesting ideas, etc.

Compositor, Fat Box, Inc
Michael Derrossett: Everybody is different, if you submit a reel and you get rejection letters, don't take it personally because

believe me people look for different things all the time. I personally look for things that aren't too obvious, kind of seamless. If its artistic, well designed and well done, it's a great thing. If its flashy and cheesy, its like "whatever."

Freelance Character Designer
Greg Dyer: Variety, to show a range is a good thing. Its good to get an idea of what the original concept was and get some kind of description of what the character was supposed to be.

Compositor, Independent
Scott Metagr: Rotoring is the biggest thing and important. It's pretty much what you start with as a Compositor is rotoring. Rotoring and masking out things is pretty much the same thing.

Clay Animator at Will Vinton Studios
JR Williams: A high quality of animation, that is animation that is done smoothly and that was realistic in the sense of movement. And I don't mean ultra-real because a lot of animation is cartoony and real kooky things happen its just a sense that what you're seeing is really happening and the animation isn't crude or jerky or amateurish looking. Here they would really put emphasis on characterization, are you able to tell who the character is by the way it moves, does that tell you something about the character rather than the situation the character is in, and I am sure there are other things as well, a general sense of sculpting ability or design ability and the ability to tell a story, the ability to just bring life into the characters.

Producer of Film and Video
Ed Royce: I look to see diversity in work, production value, so I look to see did their potential, efficiency, and effectiveness increase and rise in different types of projects and different

budgets. And I really look for diversity and availability. You got to be available and have a very diverse background. So if someone comes to me and says "I'm only available on Tuesdays and Thursdays from this hour to this hour," I say "see you later." If they come to me and say "well, I really haven't done anything" then I say " well you need to find a mentor and go get yourself in an internship program."

Production Manager at APC Studios

Maria Boltze: Good quality work, with an attention to detail There's nothing worse than good-looking work with a typo. As well, variety as I mentioned earlier. Experience in a little of everything. Also, an honest assessment of participation on each project represented on the demo reel. Which parts they did and which they had assistance with.

Animatronics Engineer at Henson Creature Studio

Vinnie Deramus: Ability that they can make something work fluently and believably, and build something efficiently using as few things as possible.

NonLinear Editor International Film and TV Workshops

Heather Fryling: Whether or not they can edit well, using different effects, doing a lot of L-cuts, making it look really well presented, the more you do the too confusing it is, but if you're an editor you should be able to see the different jump cuts and stuff.

Animator at Ball n' Chain

Chuck Jepson: Basic skill levels, I don't expect anything too extraordinary because we train people here, so I expect entry level.

Director of Animation at Disney Interactive

Tim Decker: In reels it's nice to see walk cycles, simple walk cycles, and then run cycles. Things they've worked on in other films, I don't mind seeing that process of working, what took them to get there, you know by how they were drawing, how they were thinking, how they did the storyboards, thinking about their shots. But I really look for a strong drawing skill.

Linear Editor at MVI Post

Bill Holenstein: Demo reels are actually really tricky for editors, because what happens is a lot of demo reels, all they are is graphics, and you don't know who did the graphics, you don't know if they had any hand in them, don't know who composited the graphics together. The reels are hard to determine who's good and who's not, but I think if it looks professional and look like a complete package, everything ties together with some kind of theme.

Brian Cox, Linear Editor at Atlantic Video

Brian Cox: A variety of things, different types of shows. Maybe a music video, a corporate video, different flashy things as well as simple everyday interviews, cutting back and forth between talking heads. Timing, composition, creativity, originality, basic abilities.

Video Art Director at Century III Universal Studios

Craig Stickler: Someone who has a very good sense of the overall package, details are important but if you don't present a complete package, and what I mean by that is a video that may start slow or end too quickly, the music is not in time with what's happening on the scene. If you don't feel that there's a natural flow to the imagery and if it feels like its just kind of tagged together. It is more difficult to chose someone like that than if you have a sense of timing and flow and just so the complete package just feels like its right, now there maybe some rough edges on some of the graphics and some of the elements but if its scripted properly, the images don't seem too long, the don't seem to short, the motion is too fast, if its natural, it seems like a complete package, then that's what I would look for.

Director of Traditional Animation at Animagination

Bill Railey: See how well they animate, see how well they can mimic various different styles, see figure drawings (just a bunch of naked people on paper), if you can draw them and make them look convincing then you can probably draw cartoon characters as well.

Head Illustrator at Top Hats and D'tail

Bill Britt: Want someone who has experience with logos, distilling images down to graphics essential, clean images, photorealistic rendering, total competence on the computer and can whip out whatever you want, graphic designing competencies, kindly except all kinds of jobs and can get interrupted all day long.

Technical Director of Animation at Century III Universal Studios

Ed Gross: For anyone in animation, it's hard to quantify what makes a good piece of animation or what makes a bad piece of animation. A lot of that is anything you would learn in a cinematography course, and understanding the principals of animation for one thing, and being a good modeler, knowing lighting. Just like film, computer animation is a convergence of a whole lot of disciplines. You have lighting, acting, color theory, staging composition like in painting, its all there, and it's all just as important as in film. Computer animation is just an outcropping of film, to think of it in any other way, unless you're into experimental mediums, is detrimental. A lot of mistakes that people make, especially beginners, is they assume that they can break all the rules, and one of the reasons that they assume it or don't even assume it, is cause they don't know the rules or have never learned the rules of traditional filmmaking or traditional animation. So it's important to have a good background in film and photography.

Glossary

2D Graphics
Images that utilize only two spatial coordinates, height and width (x,y).

3D Graphics
Images that utilize three spatial coordinates, height, width, and depth (x,y,z). Creating 3D Graphics is the process of creating three-dimensional models within the computer's memory, setting up lights and applying textures. After you tell the computer the angle from which you want to view the 3D scene, it will generate an image that simulates the conditions you have defined. 3D animation involves setting up the choreography, or movement, of the 3D objects, lights, and cameras.

AI
Artificial Intelligence

Animation
The illusion of movement caused by rapid display of a series of still images. When each image differs slightly, and the images are viewed at speeds of over 10 images per second, the eye perceives motion.

Animation Camera
A motion picture camera with single frame and reverse capabilities. Often this camera is mounted on a crane over compound.

Animator
An artist who uses the techniques of frame-by-frame filmmaking to give his artwork the illusion of movement.

Assistant Animator
The artist responsible for the drawings that fall between the extreme points (see key frames) of movement.

Audio
Sound related, as in audiotape, audio track, or audio file.

Background

The area of a screen or frame over which images or objects are placed. The background is the most distant element in composite layering. Backgrounds can be flat pieces of artwork that serve as the stetting for animated action. In animation, backgrounds can vary from realistically rendered scenes to sheets of colored paper. Abbreviated as BG or BKG.

Blue Screening

A process used to blend together two or more images. Best known for its use during weather broadcasts, blue screening works by placing an actor or image in front of a blue screen. Blue elements in a blue screen image are replaced with another image, known as the background. Blue was originally chosen because it best contrasts with skin color, but green and red screens are used as well.

Cel

A thin flexible, transparent sheet of cellulose acetate. Finished drawings are transferred, either by inking or xerography, onto cels. The drawings are painted on the reverse side. Also see cels.

Cel Animation

Also called traditional animation. In traditional or cel animation figures are drawn, transferred onto cels, painted, placed over a background, and photographed frame-by-frame.

Cels

Trade jargon for celuoids. There is a mistaken belief that the acetate sheets are made of celuloid.

CGI

Computer Generated Imagery. A description commonly used for visual effects and other animation productions.

CGI

Stands for Common Gateway Interface. CGI is a programming language that enables you to use forms on your Website.

Channel

One type of color information stored within an image. True color images have three channels: red, green and blue.

Character Animation
The art of making an animated figure move like a unique individual. Character animation involves the creation of "living" characters, either by traditional or computer generated animation.

Checking
The step in production in which all elements of a scene are examined and checked against the exposure sheet to ensure they are correct before being filmed.

Clay Animation
An animation technique involving the use of pliable clay figures that are manipulated before each exposure. Also called claymation.

Claymation
A term used to describe a stop motion animation technique using sculpted clay. Will Vinton Studios trademarked this animation process as Claymation. Popular claymation characters created studios include Gumby, and the California Raisins of 1988.

Composite Video
A video signal in which the color (chrominance) and brightness (luminance) information has been combined into a single signal.

Compositing
The process of digitally merging two or more images to create a final image.

Computer Animation
A field of animation that takes advantages of the computer's ability to direct and generate a video image based on preprogrammed input.

Computer Graphic
Any and all images that are digitally generated by a computer.

Conceptual Storyboard
A series of illustrations used to tell a story or present an idea. Storyboards often function much like comic books in their presentation of ideas. They are used to develop the basic visual

ideas such as the actions of the characters, the camera positions, the timing of motions, and the transitions between scenes

Creative Team
The group that developed the concept and the visual treatment of a project. Usually represented as a design studio, communications company, or advertising agency.

Dailies
A daily review of animation work in progress. The daily is usually a chance for the animation Director to critique the work in progress.

Digital Audio
Sound or music that is stored as a series of data bits (a string of 0's and 1's) rather than as a continuously varying (analog) signal

Digital Compositing
The art of combining digital video signals (as opposed to analog signals).

Digital Painting
Creating artwork on a computer directly, without recourse to traditional media.

Digital Postproduction
The process of scanning, retouching, resequencing, and compositing all the different visual images and effects. (see also postproduction)

Editing
The process of manipulating and rearranging audiovisual information into the order desired.

Editor
One who deletes or adds scenes (i.e., visual content) by following the instructions of the Director. The editor keeps the sound tracks in sync.

EDL
Edit Decision List

Effects Animation
The animation of non-character movements, such as rain, smoke, lightning or water.

Graphics
The visual content prepared for a production.

Graphic Backgrounds
The bottom-most layer on a Web page, usually with either a design or color that highlights the above copy. A small graphic can be tiled to create a background texture for a Web page.

In-Betweener
A person whose function is to draw in-between drawings. Usually a novice.

In-Betweens
The drawings that fall between the extreme points of a movement.

Instructional Design
The process of creating computer-aided methods of presenting information that results in learning.

Interactive Media
Types of media that allows users to control the flow of program material.

Interface Design
The process of creating the means according to which people will utilize software programs. Interface Design has to do with graphical conventions such as the shape of icons, typography, and color. Interface design also has to do with the sequencing of events, the available selection techniques, and the interplay of sound, text, and images.

Layouts
Drawings of backgrounds for each scene, which will later be rendered by the Background Artist.

Linear
Describes a medium in which content is arranged sequentially. The user of a linear must move through the material in either

forward or reverse motion. Images cannot be accessed out of sequence.

Mapping a Sequence of Images
Done by assigning two-dimensional picture files that are applied as maps to three-dimensional objects.

Matte
A black, opaque silhouette which prevents exposure for a specific areas of the film.

Matte Line
The outline of an image caused by a less-than-perfect line-up between a matte and its corresponding image.

Matte Painting
A photo-realistic background which is composited with a live-action foreground.

Modeling
The spatial description and placement of imaginary three-dimensional objects, environments, and scenes with a computer system.

Morphing
A 2D effect that transforms one image into another. The name for this technique was derived from the word "metamorphosis".

Multimedia
A form of communication combining text with graphics, page layout, video, audio, animation, and so forth.

Music Editor
An editor whose specialty is editing music tracks.

Postproduction
The work done on a film once photography has been completed. Post production can include editing, developing, printing, etc.

Production
The process of creating a visual project. Sometimes used to refer specifically to the second stage of the creation process, during which the project actually comes into being. Also, especially in

the film industry, production is another word for the film project itself, as in "I am working on a production."

Production Cel
The final result of creating animation using traditional ink and paint techniques. This is the art which we see on the movie screen. Cel Inkers transfer the Animator's drawings onto transparent acetate sheets, and cel Painters paint the character's colors on the reverse side. Each cel is then photographed against a background by a special movie film camera...typically two film frames for each cel. The word "cel" comes from "celulose nitrate," an early form of the acetate material used today. 'Vintage Production Cel' usually refers to artwork prior to 1970... it is estimated that 95% of the production artwork from prior to 1970 was destroyed or discarded.

Production Cel & Background Setup
An original production cel combined with a production background used in the final version of an animated film or short. Typically, cels and backgrounds may be matched after the filmmaking process for aesthetic reasons. A Keyed Setup is the production cel and the production background matched together as used in the filming of the scene. This is extremely rare, since there may be hundreds of production cels used to film a scene which uses only one production background.

Preproduction
Involves all the conceptualization and planning that takes place before a computer animation project is produced.

Presentation Storyboard
A series of images used to show a detailed summary of project plans to individuals with decision making authority.

Production Storyboard
Guides the production of an animated projects

Remixing
The process of making different versions of a song using the same tracks.

Render

To create a new digital image based on transformations of existing images or three dimensional scenes.

Rendering

The process of generating the final image in the computer. Rendering takes the modeling, lighting, texture, and color data, and decides what color each pixel should be for each frame.

Rotoscope

A device patented by Max Fleischer in 1917, which projects live-action film, one frame at a time, onto a small screen from the rear. Drawing paper is placed over the screen allowing the Animators to trace the live action images as a guide in capturing complicated movements.

Rotoscoping

A form of delaying motion capture. The Frame-by-frame projection of a live-action scene in order to trace the movements of objects. A method of capturing live action one frame at a time.

SIGGRAPH

Special Interest Group, Graphics, of the Association for Computing Machinery. The largest organization devoted to computer graphics and animation.

Sound Effects

The sounds heard in a cartoon. Also the term for digitally manipulated sound.

Sound

The audio portion of a film, which consists of three components: music, sound effects, and videos (either dialogue or narration).

Stop Motion

The animation of three-dimensional objects by moving them slightly before each exposure; also called Stop Action. The method of animating by photographing the scene one from at a time and changing the position of the moving characters or objects in small increments.

Storyboard

A sequence of graphic representations, often with dialog or captions. Shows important scenes in a program. A visual interpretation of the screenplay. A series of small consecutive drawings with accompanying caption-like descriptions of the action and sound. Usually arranged in comic-strip fashion and used to plan a film.

Storyboard Drawing

Any drawing or sequence of drawings used to describe the plot of a film visually. Typically, these rough drawings depict the overall theme or scenario of a brief moment in the film. When viewed together, the Directors and lead Animators can edit the story before animation is started. Storyboard drawings are typically smaller than standard 12 field animation drawings, depending on the studio, year and production.

Texture Mapping

The process of applying a 2D image to a 3D object defined within the computer. The process is similar to wrapping wallpaper around the object.

Visual Effects Team

The group responsible for the overall production of special effects projects. This includes digital effects, stop-motion, and composited imagery (combination of live action and computer generated imagery).

COMPUTER GRAPHICS @ PRATT

Advance Your Career in Computer Graphics.

Success in the emerging field of new media and digital art depends on cutting-edge computer graphic skills. At Pratt Institute, you can acquire these skills in the following programs:

Associate Degrees in:
- Graphic Design • Illustration • Digital Design & Interactive Media

Non-credit courses and Certificate programs in:
- Computer Animation & Video • CAD & Visualization
- Electronic Illustration/Publishing • Interactive Media

New!
Take a class online.
- Career Development • Interactive Media • HTML • Dreamweaver
- Flash • Digital Video

Authorized Training Center for:
- Autodesk • Macromedia • Discreet

Call now for a Fall 2001 catalog.

Pratt
Draw it. Build it. Make it.

Pratt Institute
Center for Continuing & Professional Studies
295 Lafayette St., NY, NY 10012 **(212) 461-6040 ext. 465**
200 Willoughby Ave., Brooklyn, NY 11205 **(718) 636-3453 ext. 465**
Visit our Web site: **ProStudies.pratt.edu**
E-mail: **prostudy@pratt.edu**

COGSWELL
Polytechnical College

JUMP into Traditional Animation

(800) 264-7955   www.cogswell.edu

Q: HOW HIGH IS HIGH? A: VERY HIGH!
Where animators have gained the creative edge in "high end" animation/FX for the leading studios since 1992.

SCHOOL OF COMMUNICATION A·R·T·S

DIGITAL ANIMATION COMPOSITING MOTION GRAPHICS
Intensive training in Maya, SoftImage XSI, & 3D Studio MAX.
Placement assistance
Financial aid to those who qualify
Call for information & requirements

RALEIGH, NC
1.800.288.7442

A Higher Digital Education™

email: school@higherdigital.com
web: www.higherdigital.com

Appendix A

References, Readings, Professional Organizations, Magazines and Websites

Bibliography

Blankstein, Jane and Avi Odeni, *TV Careers: Behind the Screen.* John Wiley & Sons, Inc., 1987.

Culhane, Shamus, *Animation: From Script to Screen.* St. Martin's Press, 1988.

Henderson, Harry, Career Opportunities In Computer and Cyberspace. Checkmark Books, 1999.

Olson, Robert, *Art Direction For Film and Video.* Focal Press, 1993.

Rabiger, Michael, *Directing: Film Techniques and Aesthetics.* Butterworth-Heinemann, 1989.

Reed, Maxine K. and Robert M., *Career Opportunities in Television, Cable, Video, and Multimedia.* Checkmark Books, 1999.

Sacks, Terence J., *Animation and Cartooning Careers.* VGM Career Horizons, 2000.

Suggested Books

Cartoon Animation by Preston Blair (Walter Foster Pub; ISBN: 1560100842)

Creating 3D Animation: The Aardman Book of Filmmaking by Peter Lord (Harry N Abrams; ISBN: 0810919966)

Designing Web Usability (New Riders Publishing; ISBN: 156205810X)

Film Directing Shot by Shot, by Steven D. Katz.(Focal Press; ISBN: 0941188108)

Inquiry by Design: Tools for Environment-Behavior Research by John Zeisel

The Art and Science of Digital Compositing by Ron Brinkman. (Morgan Kaufmann Publishers; ISBN: 0121339602)

The Art and Science of Visual Compositing (Morgan Kaufmann Publishers; ISBN: 0121339602)

The Illusion of Life (Hyperion; ISBN: 0786860707)

Understanding Comics (Kitchen Sink Press; ISBN: 006097625X)

Organizations/Associations

Association for Applied Interactive Media (AAIM) State Board for Technical and Comprehensive Education 111 Executive Center Drive Columbia, SC 29210 USA 803-737-7440 http://www.aaim.org

ACM SIGGRAPH Association for Computing Machinery

1515 Broadway New York, NY 10036 212-869-7440 (FAX) 212-869-0824 http://www.SIGGRAPH.org/

Association for Multimedia International, Inc. 10006 N. Dale Mabry Hwy. #204 Tampa, FL 33618-4424 813-960-1692 (FAX) 813-962-7911 http://www.ami.org

Art Directors Club of Metropolitan Washington 1620 Greenbrier Court Reston, VA 20910 703-742-8055 (FAX) 703-742-8055 http://www.adcmw.org

Art Institute of Architects (AIA)
American Institution of Graphics
Artists (AIGA)
National Design Center
164 Fifth Avenue
New York, NY
212-807-1990
http://www.aiga.org

ASIFA
School of Communications
Lake Superior Hall
Grand Valley State University
Allendale, MI 49401
616-895-3101
http://www.asifa.org/animate/
main.htm

Cartoonists Association
113 University Place 6th Floor
New York, NY 10003
212-254-0279
(FAX) 212-254-0673
http://
www.cartoonistsassociation.com

Computer Game Developers'
Association
CGDA Main Office
960 North San Antonio Road
#125
Los Altos, California 94022 USA
415-948-2432
(FAX): 415-948-2744
http://www.cgda.org

Graphics Artists Guild
90 John Street, Suite 403
New York, NY 10038
800-500-2672
http://www.gag.org

Interactive Multimedia Arts and
Technologies Association (IMAT)
Unit 6, 37 Kodiak Crescent
Downsview, Ontario M3J 3E5
Canada
416-233-2227
(FAX) 416-256-4391
http://www.goodmedia.com/imat/

International Interactive
Communications Society (IICS)
604-473-6166
http://www.iics.bc.ca

Large Format Cinema Association
(LFCA)
28241 Crown Valley Parkway
PMB 401
Laguna Niguel, CA 92677
949-831-1142
(FAX) 949-831-4948
http://www.lfca.org

Motion Picture Screen Cartoonist
Union

National Association for
Programming
Television Effects (NAPTE)
2425 Olympic Boulevard,
Suite 600E
Santa Monica, CA 90404
310-453-4440
(FAX) 310-453-5258
http://www.napte.org

Multimedia Development Group
(MDG)
2601 Mariposa Street
San Francisco, CA 94110 USA
415-553-2300
(FAX) 415-553-2403
http://www.mdg.org

National Association of
Broadcasters (NAB)
1771 N. Street, NW
Washington, DC 20036
202-429-5300
(FAX) 202-775-3520
http://www.nab.org/

National Multimedia Association
of America (NMAA)
4920 Niagara Rd., 3rd Floor
College Park, MD 20740 USA
800-819-1335
(FAX) 301-513-9466
http://www.nmaa.org

New York National Academy of
Television Arts & Sciences
165 West 46th Street
New York, NY 10036
212-768-7050
(FAX) 212-765-5427
http://www.nynatas.org

Professional Videographers
Association of
Greater Washington, DC
http://www.pvadc.com

Society of Motion Picture &
Television Engineers (SMPTE)
595 West Hartsdale Avenue
White Plains, NY 10607
914-761-1100
(FAX) 914-761-3115
http://www.smpte.org

Suggested Magazines

3D Artist

Accident Reconstruction Journal

Advanced Imaging

CAD Master

Cadence

Catalyst

Cine FX

Computer Graphics World

Film and Video

Game Developer

How Magazine

Interactive

MacWorld

Millimeter

Mix

Print

Star Log

Vangoria

Variety

Recommended Websites

www.highend3D.com

www.vfxpro.com

www.aw.sgi.com

www.softimage.com

www.ktx.com

www.sidefx.com

www.nathan.com

www.alertbox.com

www.awn.com

www.nycartoons.com

www.studio650.com

www.newmedia.com

Appendix B

Individual Contributors

Joe Baron
Polly Bennet
Vince Bilotta
Maria Boltze
Robert Bowen
Bill Britt
Sharon Calahan
Tony Ceglio
Jeff Cif
Raquel Coelho
Michael Collery
Kellie Cummings
Brian Cox
Judith Crow
Tim Decker
Vinnie Deramus
Michael Derrossett
Dough Dooley
Greg Dyer
Carl Edwards
Sam Edwards
Jon Fedele
Nick Forte
Heather Fryling
Tracy Fullerton
George Garcia
Ed Gross
Geoff Harrison
Tom Heddon
Rick Heffner
Bill Holenstein
Jay Jacobee
Chuck Jepson
Justin Leach
Alex Levinson
Rudy Mantel

Scott Metagr
Greg Monchak
Sunil Mukherjee
Maureen Nappi
George Olsen
Lee Proctor
Bill Railey
Mike Raso
Jayraj Raval
Judson Rosebush
Ed Royce
Joe Scacciaferro
Michael Schreiber
Jeff Secifrodella
Kurt Shade
Sonya Shannon
Lisa Slater
Craig Stickler
Mark Stucky
David Tart
Dave Taylor
Jason Van Orden
Dave Walvoord
Sandra Wan
Mike Wellins
JR Williams
Boo Wong

Studio Assistance

Heidi Swenson, Digital
  Division, VA
Richard Winkler, Curious
  Pictures, NY
Lee Proctor, Waveworks, VA
Karen Spiegel, R/GA, NY
Mike Rock, Media Vision, VA
Matt Witkowski, Henninger
  Media, VA
Gigi Green

Corporate Contributors

Aquent
Artware
Audio Vision
Blue Sky Studios
CBS Animation
Curious Pictures
Digital Division
Digital Domain
Disney Interactive
Flashpoint
Henninger Media
Image Entertainment
Industrial Light and Magic
Insurative
Judson Rosebush Company
Media Vision
Modern Digital
MVI Post
Noel Mayo Associates
NFL Films
New York Giants
Page Pals
PDI/Dreamworks
Pixar Animation Studio
R/GA
Rhythm and Hues Studios
RPA
Stan Winston Studios
School of Visual Arts
Spiderdance, Inc.
TR Squared
Waveworks Digital Media
Will Vinton Studios
XAOS

Index

Other titles from
GGC Publishing

Gardner's Guide to Multimedia and Animation Studios
$39.95 ISBN# 0-9661075-8-6

This is the most comprehensive new media industry directory. Gardner's Guide to Multimedia and Animation Studios profiles hundreds of computer graphics, animation, multimedia companies in the USA and Canada. A valuable directory for professionals and students seeking to enter the New Media job market.

Gardner's Guide to Animation Scriptwriting: The Writer's Road Map
$24.95 ISBN# 0-9661075-9-4

Provides information on writing Saturday morning cartoons and animation short films. This book is user-friendly, with illustrated text that takes you through the steps necessary to create a winning script.

Gardner's Guide to Screenwriting: The Writer's Road Map
$24.95 ISBN# 0-9661075-7-8

The Writer's Road Map is for anyone who has a great script idea, but doesn't know how to write it. You will learn how to develop marketable stories, create interesting characters, construct strong script structure, pen sharp dialogue, weave interesting themes, and write original scenes. This book provides building block exercises to help you identify the story elements in other films, and strengthen the development of your own screenplay.

Gardner's Guide to Internships in New Media 2004
$34.95 ISBN# 1-58965-008-5

This book profiles hundreds of companies and studios that offers internships in new media: Computer graphics, animation and multimedia. This book is written to prepare and guide students to internships in new media.

G G
C
®
GGC publishing

Gardner's Guide to Internships @ Multimedia and Animation Studios
$29.95 ISBN# 1-58965-000-X Pub

Profiles hundreds of computer graphics, animation, multimedia companies in the USA and Canada where internships are often available. Researched categories includes: areas of specialization; number of employees; description of company achievements, mailing address, phone and fax numbers, web address, preparing resumes, portfolios and demo reels.

orders@ggcinc.com

Gardner's Great Animation Show
ISBN: 0-9661075-4-3
UPC: 8-04619-20013-0

Entertainment for the entire family, education for the student of animation-An inspiring collection of award-winning animation short films by students from some of the best Universities and Colleges in the United States and Canada. A unique demonstration of the talent of student animators.

E-mail: info@ggcinc.com
www.GoGardner.com
Phone: 703-354-8278
Toll free:1-866-GoGardner

Its the simple truth

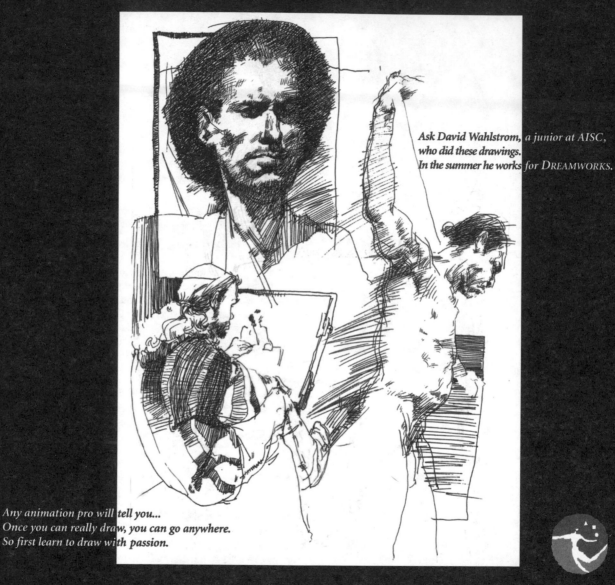

Ask David Wahlstrom, *a junior at AISC,* who did these drawings. *In the summer he works* for DREAMWORKS.

Any animation pro will tell you...
Once you can really draw, you can go anywhere.
So first learn to draw with passion.

ART INSTITUTE *of* SOUTHERN CALIFORNIA

2222 LAGUNA CANYON ROAD • LAGUNA BEACH, CALIFORNIA 92651 • 800.255.0762 • WWW.AISC.EDU • ADMISSIONS@AISC.EDU
BFA DEGREES IN
CLASSICAL ANIMATION - TRADITIONAL/COMPUTER
GRAPHIC DESIGN/DIGITAL MEDIA, ILLUSTRATION
DRAWING, PAINTING, & SCULPTURE